EXECUTIVE TALENT

Developing and Keeping the Best People

ELI GINZBERG
editor

John Wiley & Sons

NEW YORK • CHICHESTER • BRISBANE • TORONTO • SINGAPORE

658.4
E 962

Library of Congress Cataloging-in-Publication Data:

Executive talent : developing and keeping the best people / Eli Ginzberg,
    editor.

        p.   cm.
    Bibliography: p.
    Contents: The new world of work / Eli Ginzberg — Human resources
in the large corporation / George Vojta — Human resources in
strategic planning / Boris Yavitz — The human resources function /
Stephen Drotter — Restructuring for productivity / Kirby Warren —
Managers through time / Douglas W. Bray — Executives in four fields
/ John T. Dunlop — Corporate leadership and the public weal /
Mitchell Sviridoff and Renee Berger — Tomorrow's executives:
findings and directions for research / Eli Ginzberg.
    ISBN 0-471-63422-0
    1. Executives.   2. Executive ability.   I. Ginzberg, Eli, 1911–

HD38.2.E94 1988
658.4'09—dc19   87-24946
                                                                CIP

Contributors

Renee Berger
President
TEAMWORKS, Inc.

Douglas W. Bray
Chairman of the Board, Development Dimensions
International
Director–Basic Human Resources Research, AT&T
(retired)

Stephen J. Drotter
President
Drotter Human Resource Institute

John T. Dunlop
Lamont University Professor Emeritus
Harvard University

Eli Ginzberg
A. Barton Hepburn Professor Emeritus of Economics
and Director, Conservation of Human Resources
Columbia University

Mitchell Sviridoff
Professor, Urban Studies
New School for Social Research

George J. Vojta
Executive Vice President
Bankers Trust

Contributors

Kirby Warren
Vice-Dean and Professor of Management
Graduate School of Business
Columbia University

Boris Yavitz
Paul Garrett Professor of Public Policy and Business
Responsibility and Director, Management Institute
Graduate School of Business
Columbia University

Preface

This volume was prepared in response to a suggestion initially advanced by Professor Donald Lehmann, a member of the board of the Career Center at the Graduate School of Business, Columbia University, at its spring meeting in 1986. Professor Lehmann believes that, in addition to initiating and financing discrete studies of changes in corporate personnel policies and organizational structures, the Career Center should seek to contribute to the realm of ideas and theory in a way that would help young investigators.

My fellow board members were so enthusiastic about such an undertaking that I volunteered to prepare a book to be titled *Executive Talent: Developing and Keeping the Best People* by inviting chapters from knowledgeable academics and practitioners. At that time it was agreed that when the volume became available, it should serve as background reading for a conference of young researchers who would be invited to explore the themes that the book's contributors had singled out as harbingers of important future developments.

I knew that it would not be easy to persuade those whom I hoped to invite to add to their commitments and provide a completed chapter by year's end. I am pleased to report that I had only two declinations, and that all who accepted completed their work within the stipulated time. I am indebted for this evidence of friendship and commitment.

Ruth Ginzberg edited the contributions.

Eli Ginzberg
March, 1987

• v •

Contents

CHAPTER ONE

The New World of Work

ELI GINZBERG

By nature I am a skeptic; I am reluctant to see the future as radically different from the present or the recent past. In fact, I have repeatedly challenged the prevailing view that Americans have turned their back on the work ethic or that in the Vietnam era graduate students differed dramatically from their earlier counterparts. Even after my 52 years as a member of the faculty of the Graduate School of Business at Columbia University, I cannot find sharp distinctions among the succession of students I have instructed. The fact that many who were in graduate school in the late 1960s sought to avoid the draft did not appear to evidence a lack of career motivation.

When I argued with proponents of the theory that we have lost our work ethic, I sought to remind them of two simple propositions: First, people living at the margin of subsistence are likely to work very hard, not because they consider hard work a virtue but because they find it a necessity; second, most people seek to increase their income in order to enjoy a higher level of consumption, including more leisure. The amazing fact in our post-World War II experience has not been a decline in the work ethic but the remarkable stability in the work week, which has continued to hover at around 40 hours.

Nevertheless, major changes are under way in the world of work and even more loom on the horizon. Before we focus on tomorrow's executives, let us identify and assess the changes that are occurring in the work environment within which tomorrow's executives will carry out their multiple responsibilities.

FOUR MACRO FORCES

First we must define "executive." An oversimplified defini-tion is "a senior official in an organization who is responsible for helping shape its policies and determining the use of its resources to assure that its goals are accomplished and that its future growth and well being are enhanced." Executives are senior managers with broad responsibility for a significant sector of the organization or for the organization as a whole, as is the chief executive officer. Some executives are leaders in the sense that they have the capacity to alter the structure and function of their organizations in ways that add significantly to current performance and future prospects. But by definition the number of "leaders" is much smaller than the number of executives.

1. Internationalization of Business

To return to the changes occurring in the world of work, we can see that we are in an early stage of the process of accelerated internationalization. Executives in business, government, religion, universities, and other sectors must acquire, use, and update information about developments in nations far distant from their own if they are to shape and direct effectively the organizations they lead. Many of our largest corporations have demonstrated how badly they lag behind competitor export-oriented countries. Moreover, the 1986 Iran/Contra scandal points to shortcomings in U.S. foreign policy decisionmaking. Despite the passage of a new immigration law in 1986, there is no national consensus about the numbers and types of new immigrants we should admit. And only a few among the scientific leadership recognize how dependent we have become on graduate students from abroad, particularly in engineering and the natural sciences.

A few of us remember that one of the arguments used by Dwight D. Eisenhower's friends and advisors in 1951–1952 to persuade him to run for the presidency was an urgent necessity to contain the isolationist wing of the Republican Party, to insure that Robert A. Taft would not capture the nomination and possibly win the election. American isolationism may be dead, interred by the reality of superpower confrontation and the threat of nuclear extinction. But the United States still has a long road to travel before its leaders in every major sector become attuned to the growing importance of international forces.

2. Technology Revolution

A second major force that will affect tomorrow's executives is the increasing power of computer communications technology that has already transformed an entire industry—financial services. This technology may well alter the structure of organizations, both public and private, and the ways in which they operate; it redefines the skills of successive layers of employees from new hires to those at the top; and for the first time in the world's history it may tap into the human resources of persons thousands and tens of thousands of miles from the center of the organization's operations and integrate them into the ongoing processes of production.

The fuller penetration of such a powerful new technology waits upon the greater readiness and openness of newcomers to the labor force, as well as the retirement of older managers and executives to whom the new technology represents more threat than opportunity. It follows that tomorrow's executives will be more computer literate and their decisionmaking increasingly enhanced by their new competency. Henry Kaufman, Salomon Brothers' senior bond expert, recently remarked that if he is away from his office for a fortnight, he finds on his return that his younger computerwise colleagues have designed and introduced several new financial packages in his brief absence!

3. Government's Role

Although Ronald Reagan was deeply committed to shrinking the role of government, particularly the federal government, his budget request for 1988 exceeded a trillion dollars, a new high in U.S. history. Total government spending for 1987 approached 40 percent of GNP. We must not, however, assess the growing importance of government solely in expenditure terms, important as that is, because government also has an extraordinary impact on the economy through taxes, trade policy, and subsidies.

Decisions made by government will determine whether human life will continue on this planet. These decisions will determine the quality of the environment, the health of the people, the vitality of science, advances in technology, the productivity of the economy, progress toward greater equality of opportunity for the disadvantaged, the basic freedoms of the citizenry, and still other major facets of life today, tomorrow, and the day after. Politicians and bureaucrats are constrained by their obligations to their constituents and by traditions and precedents.

Tomorrow's executives in whatever sectors—business, communications, health, religion, trade unions—will have to concern themselves increasingly with government in the hope and expectation of influencing it to adopt favorable policies, to avoid adopting unfavorable policies. The ability of organizations to flourish and grow will depend in no small measure on how well they carry out their "external role." Reginald Jones, the former CEO of General Electric, once remarked that he spent more time in Washington than in his company's headquarters in Fairfield, Connecticut.

4. Organization and Management

One of the challenges that tomorrow's executives face is creating a new form of organization and management that will increase their potential to respond effectively to the changing realities in the external environment. They also will have to determine how best to utilize the human resources through which they pursue their goals and how to reassess periodically the appropriateness of those goals in light of new opportunities and threats. Regardless of the organization's track record, if the senior executives do not modify and alter it in response to the changes that time brings in its wake, the organization will slip. This is evidenced by the history of political parties in this country, in particular the almost 20-year dominance of the Democratic Party from 1933 to 1951; the brittleness of the universities in the late 1960s under the pressure of student protests; the segregated South, which was forced to change its ways in response to black protests and federal interventions; the unresolved tensions between the American Catholic hierarchy and the conservative leadership of the Pope and the Curia; the loss of balance in many academic health centers when their dollar flows became constrained; and, finally, the decline in influence and impact of major private foundations with a long and distinguished record of accomplishment.

It is not easy to alter organizational and management structures at the same time that most of the effort of executives must be directed to daily operations. But the executives who do not address the challenge when the first signs of unresponsiveness become visible are likely to pay a higher cost—a cost that in extreme cases may lead to shrink-age, merger, or even the disappearance of their organiza-tions. The increasing dynamism of external and internal environments points to the greater attention tomorrow's executives will have to give to keep their organizations and management structures attuned to new challenges and opportunities.

One of the correlates of a world whose parts are in-creasingly interdependent and that has a number of spe-cialized institutions (which reflect in part the gains from specialization) is the growing importance of communi-cations. This is the result also of the presence of many organizations with employees or members totaling in the tens and hundreds of thousands, and in some areas—such as politics and religion—in the tens and hundreds of mil-lions. The effective use of the media is the only way in which executives can keep in touch with their principal and peri-pheral constituencies. No executive, no matter how tal-ented, can hope to accomplish anything of enduring impor-tance except by eliciting and maintaining the support of interested and concerned followers. Such support depends on the strength of the images and messages that the execu-tive is able to transmit.

Words are not the only means to link the executive to the organization's membership. Action speaks louder than words; the infantry quickly learns whether its general is gung ho to capture territory or whether he seeks strategic gains with minimum casualties, as MacArthur did. The poor and the downtrodden need only a little time to distin-guish the politician who promises a lot but does little and the less skillful communicator who makes life a little better for them.

The sizable body of academic literature on corporate culture is a powerful reminder that top executives who pay attention to the basics of interpersonal relations and are sensitive to that which is really important to their employees—such as job security, promotion based on merit, the freedom to speak one's mind, the discouragement of politicking, ignoring differences based on gender, race, or other social characteristics, reasonable pay and good benefits—are likely to have a cooperative workforce. Effective written, oral, or video communications can merely reinforce the basic relation between those at the top and those below.

Over the past six years we have heard repeatedly that good television presence is critical for a presidential candidate. But of the five presidents elected since Eisenhower—Kennedy, Johnson, Nixon, Carter, and Reagan—only Reagan can be described as having a superior television presence.

FOUR HUMAN RESOURCE DIMENSIONS

Communications is the bridge linking the four major macro forces to which tomorrow's executives must be sensitive—internationalization, technology, government, and organization and management—and the four human resource dimensions that relate to these forces—educational preparation, the changing role of women, the claims of minorities, and the changing values and lifestyles of the groups that comprise the polity. Let us briefly consider each in turn.

1. A Better Educated Workforce

Sixty years ago when I graduated from high school, fewer than one in 20 of those my age graduated from college. Over 40 percent of today's high school graduates enters a 2- or 4-

year college and over one in four graduates from a 4-year college. In World War II, functional literacy was equated with the completion of four grades of elementary school. An individual was inducted into one of the Armed Forces if he or she could read a few simple signs such as "fire" or "danger," calculate his or her pay, and write a 3-sentence letter home stating he or she was well. Today, most large employers automatically screen out all applicants who are not high school graduates; and the Armed Forces accept only a small number, about 5 percent, of young people who have not obtained their high school diplomas.

The foregoing is only part of the evidence of the rising level of educational background of the American people. The other part relates to the increasing numbers and percentages of young people with advanced degrees in engineering, business, law, or the social and the natural sciences who seek and obtain positions on the managerial ladder, many with hopes and expectations of rising to a high executive position. A young man or woman who devotes between six and nine years beyond high school to prepare for a career clearly will not accept being treated as an automaton assigned to a job with narrow responsibilities, under tight control of a superior, and advanced in lockstep with others who joined the organization when he or she did.

Among the challenges that confront tomorrow's executives, the one of greatest moment is learning how to hire, assign, train, and promote the well educated younger people who today comprise the pool of management trainees and specialists. Since profitability depends on securing and maintaining competitive advantage, and since competitive advantage is in turn heavily dependent on innovation, the overwhelming challenge facing business executives is to tap more of the potential of the better trained young people than has been tapped in years past. We do not denigrate the importance of financial capital when we emphasize that the essence of corporate success is the effective mobilization of the human resources pool, particularly the executive and managerial personnel.

There are strong *a priori* grounds for believing that the successful utilization of an organization's human resources requires many prior and concomitant adjustments, including how the organization is structured and managed, the effective exploitation of new technology, reassessment of the critical buy–make alternative, and above all else, the redesign of job assignments so there is a better match between each employee's capability and performance goals. We know that tomorrow's executives will not find it easy to accomplish these tasks. They can succeed only if they accept the difficult tasks of restructuring their organizations and redesigning how work is performed, and devolve responsibilities to those closer to the market. But if they do not move early and strongly, their enterprise may not survive.

2. Impact of the Women's Movement

During the past two decades, a second stage in the women's movement has been felt in the increasing numbers of women who have opted for higher education and a career either in lieu of or in addition to marriage and motherhood. There are more women students in college than men; and, during the past few decades, the increase in women students in graduate schools of law, medicine, business, and engineering has enabled select institutions to maintain and even improve the caliber of their student bodies.

World War II, with its demand for workers in defense plants, was a watershed for the women's revolution. The second stage of that revolution arrived around 1970 when many young women for the first time sought professional and managerial careers in arenas previously closed to them—such as business, politics, government, the ministry—in fact in almost every sector of human endeavor, from astronautics to a seat on the Supreme Court.

There is no agreement among feminists, their friends, or their critics about evaluating the record to date. While the evidence shows that the number of women who hold middle-ranking jobs in a wide array of organizations has increased, relatively few have made it to the top. There is an occasional woman CEO of a large corporation but only one among the Fortune 500; a few governors, senators, ambassadors; one unsuccessful candidate for vice president in 1984; a few more have reached the top in important voluntary organizations and major foundations. Friends and critics alike counsel the dissatisfied feminists that they must allow more time to pass—15-to-20 years is only half a career. Others note that the number of attractive posts at or close to the top are relatively few and are competed for intensely.

There is scattered evidence that some women who opted for a managerial and executive career have had second thoughts about the trade-offs they had to make—the remorseless pressure of time, delaying marriage, foregoing motherhood, and marital tensions among them. In any case, these uncertainties are not likely to reverse the strong trend that for the first time has opened good career opportunities to millions of women.

The rate of women's participation in the labor force has been climbing steadily; it is currently approaching that of men. Therefore, tomorrow's executives must address more directly, intelligently, and constructively the ways in which they can make more effective use of women workers, managers, and executives. With a few outstanding exceptions, their predecessors only followed government and public pressures to lower and remove barriers in the paths of ambitious women, but seldom saw these fiats as opportunities that could strengthen their organizations and make them more effective in coping with the challenges of an uncertain future.

Even if tomorrow's executives were to adopt a positive approach to female careerists, they would have to pursue policies that extend beyond their women employees. Most adult women who are full-time employees are married, and a high proportion of them have minor children at home. Accordingly a significant change in the quality of their working lives and careers must be explored within the expanded parameters of their total roles as wives, mothers, and participating citizens in a democratic society. Today's executives recognize the problems engendered when they wish to relocate an employee in a two-worker family. But tomorrow's executives will have to expand their understanding of hitherto neglected problems that stem from the multiple roles and responsibilities of women workers.

3. The New Majority

In addition to adjusting to the large-scale increases in the number and proportion of career-oriented women, tomorrow's executives will face challenges from minorities, both native born and immigrants. In the early 1980s, a dramatic change in the long-term characteristics of the U.S. labor market occurred: For the first time in the nation's history white male workers became a minority of the total workforce. Women, native-born black, Hispanic, and other minority males, and non-white male immigrants together comprise the new majority.

This shift, which is likely to become even more weighted in the direction of the new majority in the years ahead, will be a challenge to tomorrow's executives for a number of reasons, some of which follow.

In the more than two decades since the passage of the Civil Rights Act of 1964, most large and many medium-sized organizations in both the private and public sectors have moved to hire and promote qualified minority employees. Certainly employers could have done more, but the data prove unequivocally that minority workers with educational credentials—a high school diploma, an associate's, bachelor's or master's degree—have encountered much less discrimination than their earlier counterparts. The lowering and removal of the remaining discriminatory barriers in the employment arena will be tasks for tomorrow's executives.

In addition, tomorrow's executives will face increasing pressures from the following trends: The increase in the number of young people from minority groups relative to whites who will enter the labor force in the decade ahead when the overall number of native-born entrants will be declining. Instead of a ratio of blacks in the population of one to ten, blacks and Hispanics together will account for one in every four new native-born applicants for work. And because of the uneven distribution of these minorities, with heavy concentrations in a relatively small number of major cities, they may account for as many as one in every two or three new entrants into the available labor force. Organizations located in the large cities of the South as well as in Los Angeles, Denver, Chicago, Philadelphia, New York, and other metropolitan centers outside of the South face shortages in the number of young workers they are able to hire because so many black and Hispanic youth, between one-half and one-third, have not earned high school diplomas and are therefore difficult to absorb in a service organization that requires of its employees a reasonable command of basic skills of reading, writing, and numeracy.

Today's as well as tomorrow's executives clearly must address this educational deficiency, because undereducated youth who cannot make the transition to the world of work are likely to engage in crime, add to the welfare rolls, and be an unstabilizing influence in the community—all dysfunctional to the well being and growth of business and other organizations. The challenge presented by the growing numbers of poorly educated minority youth is further compounded by the changing contours of our immigration policy. For the half century between the outbreak of World War I and the revision of the immigration quotas in 1965, the flow from abroad was radically reduced from the million or more arrivals per year that characterized the first decade of the century. Moreover those who were permitted to enter the United States were primarily persons who had been born in Europe, particularly western Europe. The quotas for the rest of the world were severely constrained.

Since 1965 the immigration picture has been changed radically along a number of axes that should concern tomorrow's executives. Among the changes are: (1) the much larger numbers who are admitted legally each year—over half a million; (2) the sizable numbers of illegal immigrants—the disputed figure is between 300,000 to 600,000 per year; (3) the increasing role of immigrants from Latin America and Asia—from a pre-1965 level of 15 percent of all immigrants to 75 percent; (4) the heavy concentration of immigrants in a relatively small number of major metropolitan areas such as Los Angeles, San Francisco, Houston, Chicago, and New York, where the percentage of foreign born among the total metropolitan population has increased and promises to increase further; and (5) the growing proportion of new immigrants whose knowledge of English is often slight.

The new immigration act is not likely to alter these trends. This implies a continuing large inflow of immigrants from non-English-speaking countries who, whatever their endowment, education, and other assets, need help to speed their acculturation. The United States has been built by immigrants, and the new streams of newcomers undoubtedly will in time contribute significantly if they are given a helping hand, particularly in English language skills. Tomorrow's executives would further their own interests if they would assist the newcomers to speed their acculturation.

The foregoing identification of a series of interrelated human resources issues—the higher educational levels of the American people, the much increased participation of women in the workplace; the growing importance of minorities (including immigrants)—helps to point up the first dimension on the human resources horizon that should concern tomorrow's executives. Simply formulated, the question is: What changes are occurring in the values and lifestyles of the population that should command the further attention of senior executives?

We are nearing the end of two decades of slow economic growth that has been associated with a distinct restriction in employment opportunities, except for certain highly educated specialists. To compound the matter, we face more aggressive competition from many parts of the world including the Far East, Brazil, and Western Europe, competition that has slowed profits and led to the dismissal of hundreds of thousands of white-collar workers, including many managers and executives. This development is new in our nation's experience. The longstanding implicit contract of lifetime employment for managerial personnel who perform acceptably has been permanently shattered. The constrained opportunities for most young academics, the anti-bureaucracy climate that has undermined morale in the federal government, the steady decline in the power of trade unions, the increasing financial pressures, and the personnel fallout facing many nonprofit institutions in the wake of cutbacks in federal funding have eroded the optimism that permeated the earlier career plans and prospects of tomorrow's managers and executives. Long-term commitment to the organization has been permanently undermined.

Furthermore, other forces that inevitably will complicate the tasks facing tomorrow's executives have begun to operate. The substantially increased formal education and training characteristic of most young people on the executive track foreshadow a growing impatience and hostility among young managers toward work assignments that do not call for the use of their talent, knowledge, and skills. With their future advancement increasingly problematic, they see even less reason than earlier cohorts to adjust to a dysfunctional environment that smothers rather than uses their motivation. Those with limited alternatives may stay put and do their jobs, but they will not invest much energy.

4. Changing Lifestyles and Values

Since more and more young and middle managers have working spouses, many of whom have serious careers, they are likely individually and jointly to develop value systems that emphasize free time and leisure activities over the demands of the workplace. Moreover, they have a different calculus from their predecessors who were willing to uproot their families and to relocate every few years if their superiors requested or required it. They are more concerned than their predecessors about the impact of such moves on their spouses' careers, and on the educational and social adjustment of their children.

Tomorrow's executives confront a truly overwhelming set of challenges. We can summarize them as follows: Within an increasingly dynamic and competitive environment, they must develop a whole new set of human resources strategies to attract and retain persons with talent and drive who are committed to new values and lifestyles. Unable to rely on their organizations for continuity of employment, promotion, and interesting work assignments, more and more young people rely on themselves to assure their future and the well-being of their family. That is the challenge above all others that faces tomorrow's executives.

CHAPTER TWO

Human Resources in the Large Corporation

GEORGE VOJTA

The human resources function in a business enterprise focuses on a universal set of priorities. Corporate effectiveness in the marketplace depends, ultimately, on the motivation and competence of the employees. The task of the human resources function is to assist senior management in managing people to achieve optimum human productivity in conceiving and executing the central purposes of the business.

These generic priorities involve organizing the work force in a rational division of labor so that the tasks in the workplace are performed successfully, establishing delegated levels of authority to assure efficiency in decision-making, designing a system to determine and communicate realistic performance objectives, and to act as a feedback mechanism for evaluating employee performance; and finally, creating an equitable process for linking performance results with rewards and sanctions so that employees believe there is a fair linkage between their performance and the rewards and punishments they experience.

Business success in the marketplace derives from success achieved in managing people according to these standards. Most would agree that these propositions apply to the large and small firm alike.

There is an important further consideration that governs the human dimension of an enterprise, and that is the business context in which the firm functions. Success in the marketplace derives from an effective presence in the markets in which the firm competes. The firm's lines of products and services must respond to customer demand; competition must be dealt with; changes in market conditions, cyclical or secular, must be adapted to. Capital and other resources must be deployed and redeployed as market requirements dictate. Success in the external markets dictates the degree of profitability and rate of growth the firm can achieve. Lack of success along these dimensions can threaten survival or lead to the demise of the business.

THE LARGE CORPORATION—
A HISTORICAL PERSPECTIVE

The large American corporation is a product of the industrialization of the U.S. economy. For a period of approximately 120 years from the mid-nineteenth century to the early 1970s, American enterprise was particularly favored by environmental conditions. Starting in the mid-1800s, the American industrial enterprise developed by exploiting production, organizational, and/or managerial technologies and leveraging these advantages progressively over a massive domestic market, relatively unchallenged by external competition. The American skill in exploiting technological breakthroughs through mass production, distribution, and financial leverage created large profitable enterprises that dominated the emerging mass markets across the continental United States.

From this base, American enterprise developed into a primary global competitive position beginning in the post-World War II period. Looking retrospectively over the whole period, it is fair to say that the competitive dominance of American business grew progressively through the two world war periods and reached its apex in the period from 1950 to 1973, ending with the first oil shock. The 1950–1973 period was characterized by the emergence of a global marketplace, and the American multinational corporation was the vehicle that exploited the opportunities inherent in the world market. It was the golden age for the large American corporation.

In 1973, the 120-year period that favored the large

American enterprise ended. The driving forces responsible for this adverse change were: progressive global deregulation of major industries and economies, the emergence of significant competition from other countries at home and abroad, the pace of technological change, the transformation of the U.S. economy to an economy dominated by services instead of manufacturing, and finally, the sudden deflation that began in 1981 and remains in force today.

The cumulative result of these adverse changes has been the competitive erosion and/or demise of many large American enterprises. At the macro level, the loss of global competitiveness has been reflected in the massive U.S. external trade deficit and the emergence of the United States as a major capital-importing and international debtor nation. At the micro level, these changes have caused a rising incidence of loss of American corporate profitability, loss of domestic and international markets, and the destruction of many firms through takeovers, mergers, and bankruptcies. (The onset of a deflationary period in 1981 hastened this process.) It is not excessive to characterize the present state of affairs in the large corporate sector of the economy as a crisis condition.

The radically altered context in which large American enterprises now compete has major implications for the human resource function in the large firm. The universal tasks associated with managing people effectively remain as high priorities, but now all of these tasks must be reconceived and managed in a prevailing hostile external context that threatens directly the survival of the firm. The implications of this hostile climate for the human resources function in the large enterprise are misunderstood and mismanaged.

The imperatives of a hostile external environment require the human resources function to focus on the relevant issue of survival and the complexity of the decision-making hierarchy of the large corporation. In far too many firms the reality is that the human resources function remains positioned in traditional fashion, staffed by technicians and oriented toward obsolete and irrelevant priorities. The objective of the human resources function in the large American enterprise must be to recapture the effectiveness of the workforce in the light of conditions that threaten the survival of the firm. This cannot happen unless the function is in total alignment with and support of the business survival strategy of the firm and is addressing the human resources implications of that strategy.

OVERRIDING ISSUES—THE BREACH OF THE HISTORIC SOCIAL CONTRACT WITH EMPLOYEES AND THE NEW ATTITUDES TOWARD WORK

All large American firms are at risk today. Many will not survive, being vulnerable to bankruptcy or takeover by others. If survival is not assured, the job security and pension rights of employees cannot be assured either. For over 100 years the social contract that governed the relationship between the large firm and its employees stipulated that in return for loyal, lifetime personal service and satisfactory job performance, employees could reasonably expect a job for life, a level of compensation that afforded them a comfortable living, and a pension that assured them of financial security in retirement.

Because of the external threats to their survival, large corporations can no longer promise to perform their obligations according to this contract. They have unilaterally abrogated their end of the contract in many, many cases. In fact, American enterprise was compelled to abrogate the contract because the loss of domestic and international competitiveness undermined the once-assured profits or resources that had allowed it to create a stable workplace for its employees.

To remedy this situation, corporate leadership must reposition and restructure the large corporations they lead to successfully adapt and cope with the pressures of deregulation, international competition, the power of advancing technology, and structural change in the economy. Such corporate repositioning ultimately involves a repositioning of the employees so that they collectively regain lost effectiveness in the marketplace. Addressing the universal priorities of managing people in the context of external adversity is the central task of senior management and the human resources professional in the large corporation today, and this must be done against the backdrop of wide distrust of the large corporation by the employees, who no longer view the enterprise as a reliable long-term employer.

Employee distrust of the large corporation has been growing for over 15 years as these untoward events have unfolded. At the same time a new attitude toward work has been defined. By and large the composition of the workforce has changed. Today, the workforce is better educated, consists of higher percentages of women and minorities, and has a view of work that requires that jobs represent an experience that contributes to their individual self-esteem and fulfillment as well as to their economic security. Contemporary employees are less willing to view a particular job as a binding relationship; they must assure their economic security both during their active work life and in their retirement. Expressions of the new attitude toward work are to be found in such phenomena as temporary, part-time, and flex-time employment; work in the home; greater job mobility; second and third careers; and voluntary early retirements and separations. Effective employees are employees who achieve job satisfaction on their own terms. This fact adds complexity to the contemporary task of people management in the large corporation.

RESPONDING TO THE ENVIRONMENT: UNDERSTANDING THE FORCES

The argument is that the human resources function in the large corporation must now focus—as it always has—on creating a workforce that causes the firm to be successful in the marketplace; but today this must be done in a context in which the firm's survival is threatened by visible hostile forces and in response to changing employee attitudes toward work.

1. Deregulation

Large American corporations were sheltered from competition by their dominance of a large isolated market and the comparative advantage deriving from the dynamics of a favorable global business environment for over 100 years. Over the past 10 years, most of these protective advantages have been removed by the progressive dismantling of trade and exchange controls and domestic deregulation of U.S. industries.

Sudden industry deregulation puts immediate adverse pressure on formerly protected enterprises. It subjects historically protected firms to new competitive pressure from more efficient entities that offer products or services of superior quality at better prices.

In deregulated industries, competitive patterns change

dramatically. A few large firms emerge to dominate the market, smaller firms occupy specialized niches, and middle-size firms either are acquired by larger firms or go bankrupt. Competing in free markets means profit margins narrow. In the end, the low-cost producer wins.

To cope with these pressures, affected firms must cut costs, eliminate inefficiencies, reintegrate operations, reduce and retrain the workforce, narrow the extent of horizontal diversification, sell unproductive assets, invest heavily in research and development of new competitive products, and generally bring all activities into focused, uncompromising alignment with the survival strategy adopted by the firm. Increased pace of decisionmaking and execution, greater intensity of work, and rigorous management focus on priorities are dominant themes and tones characterizing the firms that cope with these pressures successfully.

In companies under such pressure, the human resource function must become involved in the design of (1) the competitive strategy for survival, (2) radically simplified organizational structures to execute the strategy, (3) management of the downsizing and retraining of staff, (4) design of new, more efficient methods of decisionmaking, and (5) the setting of standards of work and reward that raise the level of productivity and morale in the workforce. There can be no delay in working on these issues because temporizing often means loss of the franchise.

Traditionally, senior management does not look to the human resources professional for major contributions on issues of this nature. Conversely, the human resources professional often has no training or experience in these areas. The human resources professional lacks the needed business credibility and business mindset. Even worse, the human resources professionals often remain oriented toward maintaining or defending the human resources system that supported the "old" company. One credible response to this problem has been to put line officers in charge of the human resources function until this alignment with the new directions can be accomplished.

2. The Globalization of Competition and Business

Large American firms must now survive in the world market against new and formidable foreign competition. The American company is now properly viewed as an enterprise managing a global business system involving the worldwide deployment of production, distribution, sourcing, finance, and other activities in multiple locations designed to optimize the firm's position in the world markets in which it chooses to compete. The workforce has now become multinational and many new types of relationships must be managed—joint venture investments, licensees, foreign staff, and so on.

Dealing with these issues requires a human resources function that is globalist in orientation and understanding. The function must be able to cope effectively with the multicultural ramifications of the global enterprise. Most of the traditional skills in the human resources function are technical and domestic in orientation. Skills in organizational design, benefits, performance appraisal, and the like have a traditional domestic context. Both the range of the new issues and the cultural context of the issues in a global enterprise go far beyond such a traditional human resources skill base. These new skills must be incorporated into the expertise base of the human resources function without delay.

3. Technology

In the new American economy, technology-driven functions—not labor—control the processes of producing food,
goods, raw materials, and services. Technology is refashion-
ing the functions of manufacturing, distribution, servicing,
and decisionmaking in business at a very fast pace. Artificial
intelligence is beginning to make significant inroads on
lower order decision-making activities in the firm. These
phenomena need to be understood, analyzed, and dealt
with from the point of view of their short- and long-term
implications for the workforce. Companies of radically different configuration and functionality (the hollowed out
corporation is an example), are emerging. These newly
configured entities will drive traditionally postured enterprises out of business.

Technology also shifts the contribution of residual labor
in business to higher value-added forms of work and decisionmaking. The concept of managing the enterprise
through strong individuals, given freedom to operate, is
coming into vogue as the prevailing management style—a
sharp contrast to the authoritarianism styles characteristic
of American business in the past. Strong people need to be
controlled in different ways. They cannot be dominated and
dictated to in classical ways. They can work with a sense of
inner discipline, but to do so they must believe in what they
do and why before they do it. Employees want flex-time,
part-time, temporary jobs. They are becoming liberated
from the boundaries of space and time in the workplace.
They work in continuous markets that never close. They are
high performance people who demand rewards based on
their measurable contributions to the firm. If they cannot
realize these things in this work environment they will
move into another one.

The human resources function must show corporate leadership the way on these matters. It must be at the forefront of understanding what is involved and translating these insights into operational responses that the leadership can understand, adapt, and manage.

4. The Structural Change to Services

Over 70 percent of all workers in the U.S. economy now work in services. A massive migration of labor out of manufacturing into the service sector is occurring. Many workers are obsolete in skills and require major retraining and/or relocation if they are to remain employable in the economy.

American labor, in contrast to that of Europe and Japan, is more mobile; but American experience and tradition in continually retraining and educating labor as labor requirements change is relatively weak. In the United States worker surplus is generally handled by lay-offs and separations. Within the firm, skill obsolescence is a major problem. An absence of worker input into decisionmaking compromises the firm's ability to adjust to these forces of change. The need to deal with these questions results from the impact of structural changes in the economy on the firm. What is required is a massive commitment to continuous training and the recycling of expertise in the face of a tradition that does not typically sanction such practices.

THE NEW ATTITUDE TOWARD WORK

The new attitude toward work requires that employees be regarded as appropriately skilled, more autonomous people who relate to their work to the extent that they enjoy it, are properly rewarded for what they do, and have the capacity to manage their own career destiny to this end. Employees of this nature will emerge in corporations that have sound business strategies to cope with the current forces in the environment. These firms are creating significant, fulfilling jobs for employees to execute these strategies. Employees in such firms buy into their jobs and willingly contribute if they experience appropriate rewards for their capabilities. They enjoy work because they are winning in the marketplace and winning for themselves at the same time. The human resources function must learn to deal with self-motivated employees, who on these terms are not intrinsically loyal to any firm. Every phase of career development must be rethought from this perspective, and employees must be communicated with effectively so they can relate to the larger priorities of the firm and "buy in." To perform this communications task successfully, human resources professionals must be in the management mainstream. Such capabilities are a major strength of Japanese companies, which compete so successfully in the world market.

THE NEW HUMAN RESOURCES FUNCTION

The traditional human resources department is populated by technical specialists who have narrow expertise in the standard menu of the human resources spectrum—salary, benefit programs, career administration, and so on. Very few human resources people have had other than home office experience or other business experience of any consequence. The age of such narrowly based competencies in the human resources function in the large corporation is over.

The standard for today's effective human resources

professional—at least at the senior level—is a technologically literate, business-minded globalist, capable of understanding and dealing with the macro and micro implications of structural change in the world economy and the issues of gaining commitment from a new breed of employee who cannot be managed by the old authoritarian standards of reward and punishment. Such people are not being grown in the natural environment of the human resources departments of large corporations. We have reached the stage at which the traditional human resources professional may have become technologically obsolete and the function is in need of being rebuilt and refocused with outside, line talent drawn from businesses that are coping successfully with the external environment.

CHAPTER THREE

Human Resources in Strategic Planning

BORIS YAVITZ

THE PAINFUL PARADOX

"Our people are our most important asset!" has become a corporate slogan, and is repeated innumerable times by most corporate chieftains in speeches, letters to stockholders, and newsletters to employees. "It's *people* who make the difference! It's the *people* who work for us who, in the final analysis, determine whether our company thrives or languishes, indeed whether it survives!"

These are not empty slogans. Much evidence has been accumulated to underscore the crucial importance of human resources to the organization's success. This has been true of American industry for some time. Today it is becoming apparent as more and more of our organizational output shifts from the production of goods to services. "All our corporate assets go down the elevator every night" has become one popular advertising agency's lament.

At the same time anyone familiar with corporate strategic planning (an exercise that develops the foundation for all corporate actions, particularly the effective utilization of its key resources), is keenly aware of how small a part the human resources specialist has typically played in the exercise.

The development of business strategies has become one of the most important functions of management in the past decade or two. In shaping their destinies most companies devote a great deal of attention, energy, and concern to the economic and technological environments in which the company operates. Similarly, care is taken to understand customer needs and to anticipate stockholder expectations. Yet very little, if any, attention is given to "our principal resource": our employees; workers and managers alike.

Here is the painful paradox. The prime mechanism for planning the deployment of corporate resources almost totally ignores the corporation's primary asset. Seldom are people resources systematically analyzed in the typical business plan, and almost never are the human resources specialists invited to take part in such an effort. True, such specialists are seldom refused admission. However, they are not invited and, by and large, they have not clamored for an invitation.

This fundamental paradox has nagged at business executives and scholars alike. The explanation ranges from the hypocrisy of the speech-making CEO, to the difficulty and ambiguity of planning human resources, to the perceived incompetence of executives who are in "personnel" departments because they couldn't cut it in a "real job."

This chapter will trace the reasons for this paradox, note some of the more recent trends that may resolve it, and conclude with a look ahead focused on the vital need for integrating strategy and human resource planning.

UNDERLYING REASONS FOR
THE PAINFUL PARADOX

From a historical perspective in many early manufacturing operations, human labor, while a major cost component, was not a particularly important determinant of production strategy. It was a commodity more flexible than most, not viewed as a key resource or asset.

Even Frederick W. Taylor, who was deeply concerned with maximizing productivity and who appreciated the significant part that labor played in its achievement, viewed the deployment of labor as a *tactical* exercise best left to plant engineers. Utilizing labor to best advantage meant having time and motion experts find the "one best way" to execute each operation, standardizing its elements and training workers accordingly. Taylor's heritage is echoed in the strategic plan for erecting a new plant, which is focused on machine design, financial pay-back analysis, and delivery schedules, while leaving manpower planning to the personnel department with specifications such as "We'll need 79 operators for the first shift and 53 for the second."

Since the beginning of the Industrial Revolution, production managers and planners have seen their role as substituting smart (or at the least, more capable) machines for less skilled human beings. Whenever the technology and economics justified the investment, machines could and should be substituted for workers. In this frame, one does not spend much time or effort weighing alternative plans for human resources.

A stronger and probably more pervasive factor influencing business thinking has been the acceptance of standard accounting conventions as useful models of reality. Consider the standard reporting convention for "our principal asset." Where in the corporate financial statement do human resources appear? Clearly not as "assets" on the balance sheet. Not even in a firm engaged in advertising, consulting, or public auditing is there any notation of its principal assets—its people. The usual recognition of employees is in the operating statement, under an expense category such as "payroll" or "wages and salaries," which instinctively triggers a managerial response to see by how much the figure can be cut to increase profits.

Worse yet, the accounting entry describing human resources is not only an "Expense," but a *"Variable Expense,"* which reveals the dominant view of the role and status of labor among the productive resources of the business. If it is an asset at all, it is a short-term one, readily liquidated when not needed, and easily reacquired if the firm needs to expand. With such an asset, who but an incompetent executive would waste his time planning its longer-term, strategic use?

In fairness to the accounting profession, it must be acknowledged that these conventions mirror our perceptions and practices, which increasingly are uniquely American. In most other industrially advanced nations—in Europe, Latin America, Japan—labor is viewed as a long-term asset and obligation of the enterprise. Whether through contract agreements, government regulations, or traditional practices, employers outside the United States cannot readily lay off or discharge employees, even when their workforce exceeds their current needs.

Without assessing the positives and negatives of the traditional American stance (for the enterprise or for society as a whole), suffice it to note that for many decades a U.S. corporation could and did treat its human resources as a variable cost and an available-on-demand asset without incurring any operating penalty. Such an environment had no place for applying strategic planning to human resources.

In many ways American unionism, even in industries in which it came to play a dominant role, has served to encourage this short-term horizon. Typically union demands have focused on "more" for the worker in terms of direct wage increases or work rule negotiations. It is only comparatively recently that unions have begun to fight for long-term job security and/or the maintenance of the size of workforce. Contrast this with many European unions that have long emphasized lifetime employment, often supported by the political parties with which they have been aligned.

American management's short-term perspective often has been criticized for acceding too readily to unreasonable union demands during upswings in the business cycle, when passing added costs on to the customer seemed an easy way out. Such excessive concessions have come back to haunt many a manufacturing company that subsequently came to be exposed to foreign competition. The results are to be found in today's Rust Belt.

Nor is the typically American perception of the short-term orientation to labor restricted to blue collar, hourly workers. The same perspective has been applied to supervisors, and even to managers and executives. During long periods of economic growth and corporate expansion, many managers viewed their current assignment as transitory.

All of the factors cited above have served to reinforce the view of labor as an easily replaceable commodity, and human resources as a short-term asset. Such a view makes long-range, strategic planning for human resources unnecessary. There have also been a number of factors that made the strategic planning of human resources very difficult.

Chief of these has been the difficulty of analyzing, measuring, and quantifying the many dimensions of human resources. While it is relatively easy to count bodies or to calculate the hourly, weekly, or monthly costs of labor (particularly at the lower skill levels), it is extremely difficult to deal with the subtle differences in knowledge, skills, attitudes, personalities, and value systems of the individuals who make up the human resources asset. Yet these are the dimensions that become increasingly important in defining the strategic options of the enterprise.

We have come a long way in convincing managers that they must recognize and be concerned with the needs and abilities of the individuals whom they manage. We have not progressed very far in describing or accounting for the qualities we seek in our workforce, nor for assessing their fair market value. It is a sobering thought that as we move up the skills ladder and as we shift increasingly from manufacturing to service operations, some basic planning dimensions become even more esoteric.

What, for example, is the "production capacity" of a bank's loan officer or an advertising copywriter? Will you double the "plant capacity" if you hire an additional loan officer or copywriter? How does one measure the "productivity" of a loan officer? Is it the number of dollars he lends, or the number of loans he makes? Is a $200 million loan to a medium sized company the equivalent of a million $200 loans to appliance buyers? And does one measure the productivity of a copywriter by the number of words she writes or the heartstrings she tugs with her prose?

At what point do we reach the limits of a worker's talent or capability (rather than a limit on the volume of work he or she can handle)? If workers can deal with complexity of the nth degree, can they cope with $n + 1, n + 3$? At what point do we decide that a "higher capability" resource is called for? These are not abstract, abstruse concepts. They are basic, fundamental concepts that every planner needs to address early in the planning process.

Some planners have complained that union inflexibility and the rigidity of work rules negate most of the benefits that strategic planning could yield. Realistically, one should structure plans around technologies, markets, product characteristics, and similar dimensions and then plug in the labor inputs under the best arrangements that can be contrived or negotiated. It is, thus, not surprising that strategic planning generally places higher priority on four "Ms" used to describe the principal productive resources of the enterprise: money, machinery, methods, and materials. They inevitably demand greater attention than human resources.

Finally, the extent to which human resources specialists *deserve* to be excluded from the strategic planning process needs to be considered. For many general managers, in a wide variety of industries, personnel managers (or persons with equivalent titles) have been viewed as only marginally knowledgeable and competent. They have been seen largely as paper shufflers who keep personnel records, interview lower level hires, and organize the annual company picnic. They were not seen as capable of providing useful information or insights into the strategic plan, and might not even understand it. Hence the current practice that calls for bringing in the personnel manager at the very end of the process, when the *important* issues had been resolved.

The general manager's view of the personnel function is not totally unjustified. In many companies it has in fact not been a very demanding one. As more sophisticated systems of compensation and benefits evolved, the function became somewhat more demanding. Earlier, only collective bargaining brought some glamor or excitement to the role. The lowly reputation of the personnel manager proved to be a classic illustration of the self-fulfilling prophecy. As the position became popularly described as a "dead-end job," it discouraged the abler and more ambitious managers from seeking it, leaving the weaker candidates to fill the slot. The weaker candidates only served to confirm the earlier prophecy of its being a dead-end job.

In recent years considerable effort has been expended in building up the competence, responsibility, and professionalism of the function. As a symbol of this transformation, the title of human resources manager has been widely adopted. While it is easier to change titles than to change the title holders' competence and esteem in which they are held, most objective observers agree that there has been a significant upgrading in the function and the quality of its practitioners. This development will be discussed more fully in the following section.

RECENT TRENDS:
SOME ENCOURAGING SIGNS

Gradually, even subtly, there has been a major change in American management's view of labor and its claims to long-term employment. Many factors contributed to changing both the perception and reality of treating human resources as a short-term, easily replaceable asset. We noted earlier that American unions began to shift their priorities in negotiations with depressed and endangered corporations. Increasingly they have emphasized job security, severance pay, and pension funding, even at the cost of give-backs in pay scales and work rule restrictions. Many companies found a surprising degree of flexibility in negotiating two-tiered wage scales, reductions in pay rates and fringes, and the modification/elimination of longstanding work rule restrictions that had limited management options and prerogatives. It follows logically that if a corporation can indeed do something about shaping its labor costs and working conditions over the next several years, it had better analyze and plan its longer term manpower needs, so as to take advantage of this newfound elasticity.

At the same time, American managers' attitudes have been reshaped by a long stream of legislation, regulations, court rulings, and changing public opinion. Nondiscrimination rules have made it difficult (if not impossible) to lay off or dismiss workers because of age, sex, race, or other characteristics. The prospect of a lengthy and costly law suit, or a banner headline, will often lead managers to accept *de facto* tenure as a more palatable solution.

American managements, as they became increasingly involved in international operations, have been forced to think about the workers they employ overseas within the host country's framework of laws and values. While they may not relish this experience, they have learned from it. When the climate in the United States began to shift in the directions noted above, experienced managers found it relatively easy to adapt. Some even recognized the favorable aspects of a long-term employment commitment, and were prepared to capitalize on it.

At the same time, a similar shift in financial reporting was taking place. For several years the professional bodies concerned with establishing accounting conventions had been struggling with an appropriate way of disclosing a company's pension liabilities on its balance sheet. A series of reforms, to be implemented over several years, emerged. Both the public discussions and the recommended steps focused managements' attention on the long-term nature of their obligations to their workforces. For some firms, particularly those under severe financial pressure, pension-funding liability became the single most important issue in their ability to sell, spin off, or even continue operations. Here was a dramatic demonstration of the importance of including human resources in the strategic planning of the business.

Two outstanding features of the business environment of the early 1980s were a severe recession and a wave of mergers and acquisitions unparalleled in recent history. Both factors put strong pressure on managements to adopt rigorous cost-containment programs, improve efficiency, and streamline operations.

The management efforts that followed often resulted in: significant cuts in manpower and payrolls, elimination of several layers of management, reductions in overhead and staff positions, and a careful review of what people do and why. Many management concluded that their optimal manpower strategy was something subtler than "a minimal head count, at minimal wage rates." Often it made sense to reduce the head count, but pay more for top performers. Keeping fewer of the better employees is a workforce strategy that demands a clear definition of the "better employee." It also means planning the corporate human resources needs in terms of quality, ability, and other dimensions beyond the traditional number of bodies and hourly or monthly rates.

Recession and intensified competition affected supervisory and managerial positions as well. Many layoffs in manufacturing companies involved staff and professional departments, as well as senior executives. The easy job-hopping era for managers had largely disappeared, and both the corporation and individual manager had to start thinking in terms of longer term relationships. In many corporations, the phenomenon of the career plateau attracted considerable attention. Promotion, the traditional method of recognizing and rewarding superior managerial performance, became increasingly difficult as company growth often came to a halt. New ways of retaining and motivating the superior performer whose career had plateaued proved to be a serious challenge. All of these factors demand more careful and longer range planning of managerial career paths, corporate executive openings, and a matching of one with the other.

An important new emphasis on human resource planning has emerged as a result of the growing globalization of our large corporations. One of the key opportunities a multinational enterprise confronts is the capability to exploit global *sourcing*. It can determine the optimal location for any of its operations. It can, for instance, carry out applied research in the United Kingdom, product engineering in Germany, assembly work in Taiwan, and recordkeeping in Jamaica. The global company can enjoy unique advantages not available to its exclusively domestic-based competitors. It is not surprising that the number of large corporations taking advantage of such a capability is growing dramatically.

The spectacular advances in communication and data processing have opened up some important new opportunities in the application of global sourcing to information handling. It is now possible to separate any portion of a complex data-processing system, via satellite communication links, and have the work performed anywhere in the world. The results can then be integrated with other portions of the system, sourced elsewhere, and recombined for use as needed at any location. A currently popular application is the exporting of data-input operations (such as key-punch entries) to Jamaica where a willing, able, and inexpensive clerical labor pool is available.

One of the most important tools in formulating a global sourcing strategy is the comparative cost/benefit analysis of different sources of labor. This implies the ability to evaluate the quality, availability, and cost of a wide range of human resources in different parts of the world, and match them against the design, production, service, and creative needs of the corporation's total mission. However, a business strategy that effectively exploits the global sourcing advantage cannot be carried out without paying close attention to the corporation's human resources. Like it or not, the human resources specialist must play an active part in determining the corporation's business strategy.

Partly because of the growing importance of this global dimension and for a variety of other reasons as well, there has been a significant change in recent years in the approach to the formulation of corporate and business strategies. Considerable emphasis has shifted from the *quantitative*, "number-pushing," aspects of the strategic plan to the *quali-*

tative attributes of company strengths and weaknesses, as well as more focus on market demands and competitive advantages. Strategic planners have grown more comfortable in dealing with the nonquantifiable aspects of the corporation's assets. They are not as ready to ignore assets simply because they do not lend themselves to easy quantification.

Another change of emphasis in the application of strategic planning that has occurred in recent years also needs to be noted. The early emphasis on the *formulation* of plans has given way to a stress on their *execution*. It became clear that good, even outstanding, planning often failed to yield useful results or benefits unless the plan was implemented sensibly. The emphasis on execution inevitably put the spotlight on *people*. It is the human resources of the organization—blue collar, white collar and managerial—that determine how successfully a plan or strategy is implemented. Strategic planning and human resources thus became more closely linked than they had been earlier.

Finally, the quality of the human resources specialist in most American corporations improved. Again, several disparate trends have contributed to this upgrading. Important advances in the study and research of human resources have been made by both academicians and practitioners. A sounder knowledge base contributes to improved practices, and these in turn attract more competent practitioners. The growing number of problems and opportunities confronting corporations along the several dimensions encouraged senior executives to assign some of their best and brightest subordinates to tackle these human resource issues.

It is becoming increasingly clear that important payoffs, both positive and negative, can accrue to the company from the way it handles its human resources. Of the several variables that can make a difference, people assets seem to be gaining a dominant position. Alert top managements have taken note of this trend and are acting accordingly. In today's climate, appropriate action consists of assigning responsibility for human resources management to the firm's most promising executives, and involving them directly in the formulation and implementation of corporate strategy.

LOOKING AHEAD: THE VITAL NEED FOR INTEGRATION

Proceeding on the reasonable assumption that the recent trends cited in the preceding section will continue to gain momentum, it seems likely that strategic planning will not deliver its full promise until it can effectively include human resources as a major organizational asset. This calls for the integration of human resources specialists and their skills with other managerial entities charged with the formulation of corporate and business strategies. Such integration requires significant additions to the attitudes and skills from both parties.

HUMAN RESOURCE PLANNING AT THE CORPORATE STRATEGY LEVEL

We will now highlight the human resource dimensions and issues that effective business strategies must deal with. We will explore these at the two commonly recognized levels of strategic planning: the *corporate* and the *business unit* levels.

Corporate strategy, as its name implies, concerns itself with issues that must be resolved at the headquarters level of a corporation actively engaged in operating a portfolio of several distinct business units. Primary attention is focused on the composition, and modification, of the businesses making up its portfolio. The following list of typical questions raised at the corporate strategy level will give the reader a better feel for this function.

What businesses should the corporation invest in? Or stay out of?

Should any new business units be added to the portfolio? Or be divested from it?

What kinds of resources should be allocated to each business? And in what amounts?

What should be the charters and general guidelines given to each business unit in the portfolio?

In summary, how should the enterprise manage its portfolio of businesses so as to achieve its corporate goals and objectives?

Taking into consideration the recent trends outlined earlier, an effective corporate strategy must be one able to deal with the human resources implications of the portfolio of businesses it operates at least as well as it assesses more conventional assets such as financial capital. These human resources assets are not only affected by the composition of the business portfolio, they also help determine its optimal shape. It is clearly a two-way relationship.

Let us begin by checking off some of the critical actions and decisions that corporate strategy must guide and direct in response to the developments previously identified as changing trends affecting the business environment:

Corporate "restructuring," "slimming down," "downsizing," divesting product lines, "spinning off" business segments.

Global sourcing of products and services, for both internal and external markets, from any part of the world where the corporation maintains (or decides to locate) facilities, to any other part of the world where its key markets are situated.

Negotiating with unions, host governments, and local workers on wage rates, labor practices, international transfers, in all applicable geographic and industry jurisdictions.

Determining current and future pension-funding liabilities the corporation is exposed to in the various businesses and jurisdictions within which it operates.

Dealing with management succession problems at the top levels of each of the principal business units, as slots become vacant due to retirement, transfer or removal.

Meeting internally or externally mandated quotas or target levels established for various demographic or work-related characteristics.

To deal with these issues, the corporation needs to aggregate large amounts of data assembled by its business units as to their respective human resources. Such data should include:

Inventory of current human resources, in as rich an array of dimensions as possible, by type of business, country, function, background, and so on.

Projected manpower needs for the next three to five years by business units and locations included in the plan.

The substitutability, transferability, replaceability of the manpower needs on hand or projected.

The lead times required to staff future needs or dispose of redundancies in the various categories of manpower.

Identification of the critical paths and likely bottlenecks in matching manpower needs with availabilities.

When such data are available by business unit, country, and appropriate human resources characteristics, it becomes possible to plan corporate activities for the next five years and be able to anticipate labor transfers, surpluses and shortages, expansions and contractions. Only then can realistic judgments be made as to the probability of achieving the performance objectives the plan projects, hence its capacity to meet corporate goals.

Besides providing for the maintenance of ongoing operations, the strategic plan must also identify actions that must be taken today to anticipate future shifts in labor needs. For example, knowing that certain scarce skills will be needed in two years has important implications for current relations with the universities or professional associations from which such skills are normally recruited. In some cases it might be necessary to continue recruiting at low levels, even when there is no current demand for the skill, simply to keep the recruiting pipelines open.

Conversely, sizable reductions or consolidations in the workforce need to be anticipated well in advance, if the costs inherent in such consolidation are to be contained. Such costs are not limited to severance pay, or other money payments. They include potential damage to government, union, and public relations, which may prove even more costly in the long run.

To put these matters in perspective, it should be pointed out that the foregoing applies the same kind of strategic analysis to human resources management that has long been applied to a simpler asset: cash. For example, in any portfolio there usually will be some businesses that will require extensive and frequent infusions of cash, while others will enjoy surpluses. Some units' cash needs will be highly cyclical, others' will remain fairly stable. Some businesses will find it easier to tap the capital markets for new funds because of their current popularity or cachet. Others will be ignored or have to pay a premium on funds borrowed.

Today's managers know how to juggle, balance and offset cash flows among business units in any portfolio configuration to provide for synergies, stability or risk containment. Highly analogous considerations should prove transferable from cash to human resources in the context of a strengthened corporate strategy.

HUMAN RESOURCE PLANNING AT THE BUSINESS UNIT STRATEGY LEVEL

This level of strategic planning is carried out by each of the business units that make up the corporate portfolio, and focuses essentially on determining the direction and shape each business will take over the next five years or more. Which particular segments of the market does it plan to serve? With what product or service lines? And what kind of an organization will accomplish this effectively?

The planning process usually consists of a two-step analysis: the external, or environmental scan; and the internal, or strengths-and-weaknesses, profile. The matching of one against the other provides the basis for selecting the appropriate domain, mission, and strategy that will give the business its strongest competitive advantage.

In conducting the environmental scan, the planner seeks

to identify the trends and characteristics that shape the markets to be served by the business. These characteristics are usually clustered under four headings: economic, technological, social, and political. To help focus attention on key factors, it is customary to summarize the analysis under a listing of perceived opportunities and threats, often followed by the highlighting of the so-called crucial factors for success. That is the handful of items that *must* be done right if the enterprise is to succeed.

Customers, competitors, suppliers, and regulators usually receive close scrutiny. The human resources of the firm rarely command comparable attention. Yet if the business unit is to formulate an effective strategy for itself and provide corporate management with the data it needs, nothing less is acceptable.

As a first step, it is suggested that in conducting the environmental scan—the economic and technological trends—the probable shifts in the *demand* for human resources must be assessed, while social and political trends serve to anticipate shifts on the *supply* side. For example, projected decreases in the price of crude oil and a breakthrough in rolling mill technology, will most likely increase the demand for skilled set-up machinists. Meanwhile, the rising cost of training and the curtailment of local government subsidies to vocational education is likely to make machinists more difficult to recruit. These are the kinds of insights likely to emerge from the inclusion of human resources specialists on the strategic planning team.

Similarly, while conducting the internal analysis, it would be extremely useful if the entries in the resultant strengths-and-weaknesses profile were translated to take into account specific human resources and the range of their capabilities. Thus the observation that "technical sales ability" is one of the major strengths our business enjoys, should be translated to mean, "We have 14 graduate civil engineers, each with a year's sales training and two years of selling experience." Here again, the aid given by a skilled human resources specialist can be invaluable.

The last step in formulating the business strategy usually deals with insuring compatibility between strategy and structure. "Structure" as used in this context covers a wide range of variables, including: organizational structures; planning and control processes; compensation, incentives, and communication systems; and leadership styles and cultures. Simply stated, the way we manage ourselves and how our unit is put together must be compatible with the mission we select for ourselves and the strategies we adopt. Our human resources are probably the key determinant of our "structure."

Finally, a well articulated business strategy provides useful guidelines for effective human resources management, by general managers and specialists alike. It sets priorities for the various functions performed by the human resources specialist, for example: When and where is it important to formalize new personnel practices or develop stronger leadership? Or design new incentive packages? Or encourage more innovation and entrepreneurship?

Our conclusions can be readily summarized. If current trends in the business environment continue, the contribution made by strategic planning to the success of an enterprise will be directly proportional to the extent that the firm's human resources are included in such planning. The painful paradox of excluding consideration of the enterprise's principal asset from its most critical planning process may be explained by a variety of historical weaknesses and coincidences. Explaining it, however, does not correct its deficiencies.

Many corporations, even today, sense that they are not receiving full returns from their investment of funds, time, and effort in strategic planning. In most cases the shortfall is traceable to ineffective implementation which, in turn, is the result of inadequate planning for and poor utilization of its human resources. All indications are that the future will prove even more demanding. It is high time that human resources managers become active participants in the formulation and implementation of the corporation's business strategy.

CHAPTER FOUR

The Human Resources Function

STEPHEN DROTTER

T he image that comes to mind when I think of the human resources (HR) function in the future world of work is *dinosaur*. There is some evidence of the function adapting to the complex changes affecting American business so the function is still alive. Adaptation to date has been much too little and much too slow to make me feel comfortable about its long-term survival. If it doesn't adapt more thoroughly it shouldn't survive.

There is still some question whether human resources is a function. One human resources manager I spoke with recently, who heads HR for a $2-billion division of a $25-billion company, insisted that HR was not a function in his company. He said there was no career in HR work, only jobs. Very few people had or were required to have expertise in any of the many HR disciplines. No one was hired from the college campus specifically to work in human resources. A few technical experts work at the corporate level.

Another $2.5-billion business that I have come to know divides its human resources work among three different senior vice presidents and the president. There is very little scope for the work of the function to be integrated or coordinated with other functions. Synergy is out. Clearly, in this company, HR isn't a function.

CURRENT CONDITIONS

The function has been an easy target for managers and employees who are dissatisfied with their job, their pay, the time it takes to fill an open job, the quality of the workforce, or the prices in the cafeteria. In the 20 years and more that I have been doing human resources work I haven't seen much improvement. If anything, the complaining may have grown even louder.

Problems in HR management have become more significant to the future of the business. Reductions in force (even the most successful and well established companies are doing it), increased international competition, management succession shortfalls, dislocations caused by mergers and acquisitions, dramatic changes in worker attitudes and values, and technology-driven obsolescence are examples of human resources problems that are now increasingly common in both large and small companies. Managers and executives who run American businesses are having a difficult time coping with these phenomena, particularly when they occur in combination. When management turns to the HR function for a contribution, it may or may not get what it asks for. It usually doesn't get what it needs. So, managers complain or ignore the function. Employees caught up in these unsettling situations also look to the HR function for help. They are even more likely to be disappointed. Why?

I believe there are several basic reasons that arise from within the function itself. The most important is that the function does not exhibit a proper attitude about its worth. Second, the HR philosophy that underlies the plans, programs, and day-to-day efforts is often obsolete or nonexistent. Third, the appropriate roles of managers, employees, and HR professionals are not clearly defined or aptly executed. I will outline some simple but powerful actions aimed at improving the current and future effectiveness of the HR function. I believe that for the remainder of this century problems in the human resources area will be *the* most significant challenge facing business. The future world of work needs an effective HR function and a different and larger contribution from HR.

1. Human Resources: A Faulty Stance

When one thinks about the functions within a business, the focus is on marketing (including sales), engineering (research technology, design), manufacturing (operations, production), finance (accounting, treasury) and human resources. It is extremely *rare* for a company to treat its HR function as an *equal* player on the business team. Yet, human resources must make a contribution to the business just like the other functions.

One barometer of the role of the HR function is pay. Human resources functional heads are being paid quite handsomely these days but not quite as well as other functional heads, such as legal and strategic planning. At the lower levels the inequality is greater. What makes the HR function different is that the functional head and the other key managers in the function don't fight for equal treatment for their people (relative to other functions). In fact, HR heads at corporate level or division/group level will battle the CEO, the board of directors, and the key line executives endlessly for improvements in pay for individuals in the other functions. But seldom, if ever, will they do battle to make the HR function equal in compensation to the other functions. If key people in the function feel that their function should be an equal member of the business team, they don't behave that way. In general, HR people do not consider themselves equal.

There is a diverse set of definitions for the function. There seem to be as many different definitions as there are companies. I have worked full time in three major corporations (as head of the HR function in two of them) and consulted with two dozen more. In addition I have been a member of four different organizations comprised solely of senior corporate HR officers, representing over 100 major corporations. There is little commonality of charter, and wide differences in authority, accountability, reporting relationships, and resources. These differences don't appear to be business- or industry-driven. It isn't clear what drives them. When HR function leaders get together, they spend time comparing programs, not discussing the effectiveness of the function. Standards for performance are hardly ever mentioned.

The greatest difference between the HR function and other functions is the staffing and technical training of functional members. Staffing the HR function continues without regard to the basic principles used in the successful staffing of other functions. Little college campus recruiting takes place for students with a career interest in human resources. People who fail in other functions are routinely accepted for the HR jobs. Banks and insurance companies still use the head of HR position as a pass-through for high potential or a holding dock for senior executives who are "stuck." Not one of these three situations—the absence of college recruiting, accepting failures, using the top job as a pass-through or holding dock—would be tolerated by engineering or marketing, let alone finance or legal.

Management training remains a neglected area but technical training has made great strides for marketing and sales, finance, underwriting, lending, back office operations, and engineering personnel. Technical training for HR professionals in such areas as assessment (of managerial talent), succession planning, program design (you can buy someone else's program but it is hard to find high quality instruction on how to build your own) is hard to find. This is noteworthy considering that HR is usually charged with designing (or purchasing) training for the business at large.

Getting HR professionals to leave their jobs for a few

days to take skill training is next to impossible. The usual excuse is that the boss might (or does) want something. It is infinitely easier to allow general managers to leave for eight weeks than to allow HR people to leave for one week. Nonetheless, there is a body of knowledge to be assimilated, a basic set of skills to be developed, and a variety of work experience to be programmed in order to build effective HR skills.

The attitude pervading the HR function is best described as one of political survival. Strive to survive, don't rock the boat, don't take too much risk. These are sure-fire prescriptions for extinction. The functional leaders may or may not agree with the programs in place, the management practices, or any number of HR activities, but they exhibit an "I want to survive" attitude and won't challenge the system around them enough to get it changed.

2. The HR Philosophy is Obsolete

Philosophies exist whether they are explicitly stated or not. Many corporations have taken time and effort to develop clearly stated and meaningful philosophies. Johnson & Johnson and General Electric are good examples. Companies that have not made explicit statements of philosophy may have mission statements or corporate purpose statements that in fact define a philosophy regarding the treatment of employees. These statements are often carried down into the business, and operating groups often have their own explicit statements. DuPont is a good example. On the other hand, there are many companies where the corporate philosophy remains implicit.

Careful examination of many corporate statements (of philosophy, mission, or purpose) reveals some common elements. Innovation, highest quality, open communication, maximum effort, customer satisfaction, cost effectiveness, and recently, excellence, are among the most popular. The value of their employees and desired methods of employee treatment, (e.g., fair, open, honest) are also surfacing.

Every HR function that I am aware of is trying to support, within its own charter, the corporate statement. Examining the underlying philosophy of policies, programs, and practices that the HR function has designed or developed usually reveals a *contradictory* philosophy. Many of the best known and most frequently used HR systems have an effect on employees that is opposite from the professed goal.

For example, compensation systems that rely on 30 or more pay grades for professional and managerial positions and have low ceilings in each grade are designed to put work into small compartments and measure it precisely. "Effort should be controlled and contained" is their underlying philosophy.

Position evaluation systems that use size of empire (number of people managed, the amount of operating budget, number of locations, etc.) do *not* support cost effectiveness. These systems have a "bigger is better" philosophy.

Management-by-objective (MBO) systems are commonly driven from the top and are built around management initiative. They are used for two primary purposes—management control of employee effort and facilitating compensation decisions. However, they result in gamesmanship on the part of employees. Don't overcommit, don't commit to any stretch goals, don't promise anything you aren't sure you can deliver are common employee reactions.

There are many other examples. Succession-planning

systems that collect employee-generated and management-generated data but where no further use of the data is ever made are contradictory. The pretense of being open, participative, and future- (career-) oriented without any substantive follow-up leaves employees and managers alike doubting the expressed value system of the organization.

Perhaps the best example of a contradictory philosophy is the proactive versus the reactive choice. It is common for HR to be exclusively reactive but never to admit it. As a result, the business is always chasing the power curve on staffing key jobs, updating compensation programs, or implementing technological changes. This leads managers and employees to be continually dissatisfied with the HR programs.

3. Role Problems

Examining the role for HR requires at least some analysis of the role of the manager or executive as well as the role of individual employees. Much HR work involves the customer in a unique way—during the design, development, or implementation of a program. This is not usually the case for other functions. For HR, the customer is almost always internal to the business. Such a relationship should put the function through a level of scrutiny that results in higher quality output. Sometimes it does, but it also leads to aberrations. The role of HR is often shaped more by the people outside it than by its own initiatives and insights.

The head of HR usually has a considerable amount of involvement with the CEO or the COO or both. The interaction may be with executive compensation, succession planning, labor negotiations, benefit changes, and reporting to board of directors on all of these issues. Delicate conversations often take place because the CEO's or COO's pay and bonus are involved. Top executive compensation becomes a matter of public record through proxy statements or business publications. The top executives want to be competitive with their peers, especially those in their own industry. Much attention is paid to the HR function head when he or she works on executive compensation. Unfortunately, the result in too many cases is that the head of HR either spends too much time on this subject and becomes a compensation analyst or becomes a valet to the CEO or COO. In either case the HR function loses time and momentum required for leadership.

Managerial effort seems to be divided into two different compartments. The first includes deal-making, customer interactions, giving orders, criticizing, gathering resources, tactical thinking, and planning. The second compartment contains the developing or training of subordinates, strategic planning, giving praise, integrating with other operating units, unstructured or employee-initiated meetings, coaching, and counseling. These compartments receive different amounts of attention. The deal-making compartment tends to receive the most time and attention. This is where the action is, where the feedback is most direct. The strategic planning compartment receives little attention. In fact, it is frequently assigned to a support group in HR.

As a result, the HR function is left with an inappropriately large role in coaching and counseling. Often it takes the form of hand-holding during periods of crisis with subordinates of a manager who is spending most or all of his or her time on compartment-one issues (deal making, customer interface, etc.). This hand-holding role can be seductive because it usually involves spending considerable time with a major power figure. It also may involve the HR person, at least tangentially, in an important business activ-

ity such as a reorganization or an acquisition when otherwise he or she might not be involved. This is hard to resist.
Fulfilling this hand-holding role may make the HR executive feel good; but it doesn't add much to the business, and
it is often hard to point to any tangible contribution.

In both of the role aberrations—being a valet for the most
senior executives or a hand-holder for their subordinates—
the HR function itself, or the senior people in the function,
come to be viewed by the rest of the organization as having
been "captured" by one or another group of senior managers. Lower level managers and employees come to develop
a fundamental mistrust for the HR function. Talking to HR
is like talking to the senior managers. Therefore, they can be
used to deliver messages. They can't be used for analysis,
coaching, or objective input on programs or plans.

For individual employees (who may also be managers)
getting recognition or reward for current effort and clear
directions for the future are critical needs. All employees
have such needs. Their managers or HR departments represent the principal sources of information and/or satisfaction. As employees press their management for satisfaction,
management frequently points them to HR. More often than
not, HR accepts this responsibility. It is appropriate for the
employee to look for and find satisfaction. As the shift from
industrial worker to knowledge worker accelerates, it is
increasingly common for the employee to know much more
about the market value of his or her work. This is particularly true in financial services and high-tech businesses.
Hence, they provide valuable market intelligence to management and to HR on the value of labor, the supply of labor,
and trends in employment systems and reward structures.

Frequently, but by no means always, management and
the HR function react with panic, anger, or hostility. The HR
role is likely to be reactive and defensive when both the

employee and the employee's manager are pushing hard for changes. It takes considerable maturity and balance to cope with such double-teaming. In any event, HR often becomes the complaint department, a thankless and nonproductive role.

The realities of the clock and calendar eliminate constructive effort if the functional head is a compensation analyst or a valet, and other functional members are hand-holding or fighting off employee and manager double-teams. It is practically impossible under these conditions for the HR function to make the necessary contribution to the business.

THE FUTURE

Even if the current business environment were to remain constant, it would be desirable for the HR function to introduce fundamental changes in its attitude, philosophy, and role. As previously noted, the foundations of HR are inappropriate and lead to less-than-acceptable contributions. But we know that the environment cannot remain stable. Consider these important changes that are currently under way:

There has been a frenzy of mergers, acquisitions, and leveraged buyouts. Restructurings and greenmail have become common occurrences. Such activities create employment insecurity, make obsolete or redundant both people and people-related systems, and create organizational chaos through the sale of assets to reduce debt. New systems for managing human resources during periods of rising uncertainty are needed. Achieving production goals, maintaining or improving quality levels, and encouraging innovation are almost impossible in such work environments. Control-oriented management systems, compensation systems that require careful measurement, and tight compartmentalization won't work in this maelstrom of moving targets.

Intense multinational competition has left the manufacturing core of American business in a cost-and-profit squeeze that requires innovation in process and product, much leaner organizations, and rapid geographic redeployment. Searching for new market opportunities has also resulted in changing the business mix—Sears, General Electric, General Motors are now major financial service companies. USX and duPont own large oil companies. AT&T, Xerox, IBM, Exxon, duPont, and the major automotive and steel companies are laying off significant numbers of employees. Early retirement programs are creating a large pool of experienced workers who possess some economic security, considerable energy, and are willing to work but many of whom are currently unemployed.

Deregulation in banking, the airlines, public utilities, and many other industries has also caused large-scale reexamination of hiring practices, labor contracts, pay practices, succession planning, and employee involvement programs. There is no end of changes in sight. The degree of instability in the environment can only increase.

For American business to cope with these unsettling conditions, it will have to become expert in managing complex human resource issues. That will require in the future, as it does now, a first-rate HR function. Past ineffectiveness coupled with these new and growing challenges make the case for HR functional change both compelling and perhaps inevitable. It makes no sense for HR to stick with current attitudes, philosophies, or roles that have failed to produce the required outputs. What changes are needed?

AN ATTITUDE OF
PERFORMANCE SUPERIORITY

To deal effectively with these complex challenges, the HR functional leaders will have to adopt a more self-respecting view of the value of their function and a fuller appreciation for its potential contribution. Striving to become an equal player on the business team won't be sufficient. The HR functional leaders will have to adopt an attitude of performance superiority and build their function accordingly. If the functional leaders don't do it, line management will do it.

Resource limitations are likely to accompany the leaner, more cost-effective management structures. There can't be room for any employee in the HR function who earlier failed in some other function. In fact, staffing the function must be done on exactly the same (or better, if possible) basis that governs the staffing of the other functions. The HR functional leaders will have to be experienced in most, but at a minimum in at least three, major disciplines (e.g., recruiting, compensation, training, development, labor relations, organization planning, and manpower planning). Recruiting for the function will have to be accomplished using the same compensation scale as comparably positioned engineers or underwriters or marketers. Training and development of functional members must be carefully planned and cover college-to-senior-level career spans. Attracting and retaining the best are imperative.

If the HR functional leaders don't adopt this attitude, they never will make the required contribution to the business. They won't be able to convince the line management of their real worth if they operate with only an "adequate" team. The HR function will continue to be excluded from work on the demand side of the human resource equation.

Performance superiority, by necessity, will involve shifting from the supply side of human resource management to the demand side. By supply side I refer to those activities that attract and retain employees like recruiting, placement, salary administration, career planning, and so on. Conversely, a concentration on how many employees are really needed, how should work be organized for maximum effectiveness, what skills are required to perform job duties, how should the business organization be restructured, is the demand side of human resources.

Many demand-side activities are at present performed by line or operating management. Some of the more sophisticated HR organizations have succeeded in becoming involved. In large part, however, HR is not involved and further is not allowed to be involved. Looking at both the supply and demand for human resources will greatly improve the effectiveness of the function. It is also important that an understanding of human systems, human behavior, and human economics be included in the demand-side approach.

Human resources professionals will require new skills. Organization design, job design, long-range manpower planning, succession planning, and greater in-depth knowledge of how the business really works are required for HR to make an optimal demand-side contribution.

Decisions are made every day, in businesses large and small, that affect the demand for human resources. Whether they are made skillfully depends on the experience and training of the decisionmakers. When executive search firms flourish, when major corporations abruptly announce 25 percent reductions in force, when technical obsolescence causes thousands of employees to be offered early retirement at a cost of hundreds of millions of dollars, it suggests that the demand-side analysis and planning are not being done very well. There is plenty of room for able contributors.

If HR professionals make the commitment to performance superiority, they will become indispensable to the business team. They are in a unique position to apply behavioral science training, employee relations experience, a focus on human systems to both the supply side and demand side of human resource management. Accepting less than the best personnel into the function, and failing to make training and development mandatory for all, will certainly lead to extinction. The attitudes of functional members, and most importantly, the attitudes of the functional leaders need to emphasize performance superiority.

A PHILOSOPHY OF SELF MANAGEMENT

Our world of work has become very uncertain. Change seems to be the only constant. Control as a basis for operations is difficult at best. Control as the basis for human resource management has become impossible. Many companies are looking for an alternative. Control-based systems are stifling and are not able to attract or retain talent. They don't foster innovation or creativity. Knowledge workers demand freedom to act. Business leaders, compensation managers, and employees alike want to be recognized and paid for their contributions.

Pay systems represent the most fertile area for a new approach. Many pay systems, for example, are still using the amount or quality of *input*. The number of people managed; the size of the budget; skill, care and effort; education or training all are common factors used to decide to which of many small pay ranges a job and its incumbent should be assigned. Pay for performance is the philosophy that accompanies the application of dollars to these systems. Small percentage increases go to every employee; slightly bigger increments go to the star performers.

Pay for contribution is needed. It calls for radical change in system design. There are systems in entertainment, sports, and on Wall Street that provide the opportunity for unusual rewards for unusual contributions.

Small salaries and large bonuses or small fixed compensation and large variable compensation would go a long way toward improving the effectiveness of the pay system to attract and retain talent. To make such a system work, a small number of pay grades, such as one grade for each management level, and two or three grades for individual contributors, must be part of the system. Each grade would need a wide range, perhaps 200 percent. Most of all, such a system would require a philosophy of self-management. The system designers and the system administrators—usually HR—must be willing to let employees manage their own effort, seek their own optimum output level, and be rewarded commensurately.

The primary work management system, management by objective (MBO) or a similar system, can encourage self-management. When Peter Drucker first wrote about MBO in 1954, he referred to it as "management by objectives and self control." He stressed self-control and indicated that the real value of an objectives system was that individuals could control their own performance and not be managed through domination. His original idea was clearly lost. He felt employees would strive to do their best rather than just

enough, and believed that they would set higher performance goals if they were self-managed, managed by self-
control. It is important to emphasize that self-management
doesn't mean doing what one feels like doing. It means
figuring out what needs to be done and then doing it.
Regular reviews with supervisors, initiated by employees,
are required. Training in how to make such a system work
is available. DuPont of Canada is actively pursuing self-
management by objective in its basic approach to managing
its business.

The leap in philosophy from control to self-management
can bear handsome dividends. It is an excellent way to
improve the management system where there are large
numbers of knowledge workers. All HR systems should be
based on this philosophy. Self-nomination for open positions up to high levels is desirable. Succession planning
would have to be closely coupled with career planning, and
individual employee input on career directions and prefer-
ences is also needed. The net effect would be an unleashing
of employee energy that would make work more fun and
more rewarding for employees and more profitable for the
business.

A LEADERSHIP ROLE AND
MORE REASONABLE SHARING OF DUTIES

A service or staff support role for HR is no longer sufficient.
Waiting to be asked doesn't make sense. Leadership is
needed. An example of a real leadership action will help to
illustrate this. The changes in demographics for people
entering the workforce by 1995 is becoming increasingly
delineated. The birthrate continues to decline; the baby
boom years were an aberration. By 1995, the age-25-to-34

population will shrink by 5 million. The 18-year-old population will be almost 40 percent below its postwar peak. At
the same time, new jobs are scheduled to increase by 15 to 25
million. Recent trends of increased female participation in
the workforce have helped to make up what would earlier
have been a serious shortfall in new workers. Their participation rate will continue to climb, but the rate of increase is
slowing. It appears that we may face a future shortfall in the
U.S. labor supply.

In addition to numbers, there is likely to be a quality
shortfall. One of every three new workers will have been
educated in an urban school system, many of which fall
seriously short. In addition, one out of four ninth graders
currently does not graduate from high school. The number
of students in the 18-to-24 year age group at the college level
will drop from about 7.4 million in 1982 to about 5.9 million
by 1992. College enrollment for persons over age 25 is
expected to increase substantially, but the academic quality
of those age 18 to 24 entering the workforce will fall short of
the prospective demand.

Harold E. Johnson, senior vice-president, personnel and
administration, at Travelers Insurance spent considerable
time analyzing the demographics and evaluating the implications. He concluded that new hires will be very expensive—cost effectiveness will be critical . . . will do more than
minimum wage ever did (to costs) for a business like ours.
He has charged senior management to:

1. Begin now to objectively evaluate and select our
   workforce of the future from current ranks.

2. Begin now to attract and retain the highest quality
   portion of the 18–35 year olds.

3. Pursue alternative sources for labor.

4. Describe the quality, skill, and numbers of people needed from now through 1995 in light of major increases in the application of technology.[1]

This is an excellent example of not waiting to be asked but rather taking a leadership role in a critical area where HR expertise is needed. Item 4 is a clear example of managing the demand side of the human resource equation. Human resources systems at Travelers are being added or changed to support this effort. This is not an easy task and going "on record" on a critical subject involves personal risk for the HR head. One can also fail to change management's willingness to introduce radical new approaches to staffing the business. But it is more likely that Travelers will meet its prospective labor supply crisis.

There is another kind of leadership role for HR related to the definition of responsibilities in executing HR programs. Management development provides an excellent example. The current wisdom in management development points to the individual as the prime mover. However, for management development to be effective, all of the following conditions need to be met: The right person must take the right program, at the right time, with the right attitude, from the right instructor, with the right application on the job. Even the most committed employee cannot control all of these variables. The manager's role is critical. That role includes the following:

Defining the purpose of the development exposure and identifying the change required is the first responsibility of the manager. The manager is in a preferred position to

[1]Memo to top management at Travelers, Inc., September 10, 1986.

make subordinates aware of the needed change and is the person most likely to be persuasive. It is important also to remember that the manager has much to gain.

Confirming the choice of program is the next key element. Program can mean a course, a new job assignment, individual tutoring, a special or additional work project, or any one of a number of other opportunities. With purpose and a goal in mind, evaluating the alternatives becomes fairly easy. The HR staff person can do the research needed to uncover the alternatives. The decision on what specific action to take, however, should not be left to HR.

Stimulating the right attitude on the part of the person to be developed can be done through coaching, incentives, and improved hiring practices, such as not hiring anyone "allergic" to learning. This is a common practice in sophisticated companies. The critical decision for the manager is whether or not to allow an employee, with no interest in his or her own development, to stay on the payroll. People do not improve by chance. Being "too busy all the time" is a sign that development is needed.

Focusing on the potential for development at the time of the job application and following up repeatedly may be the most effective role that the manager can play. If a person quits smoking for only a brief time, this will have no effect on his or her health. Reinforcement is needed. The manager is in the best position to provide effective follow-up. It may require as little as a brief monthly reminder. It could take as much as daily reviews. Whatever it takes, it is worth doing if you want your management development effort to result in significant improvement in job performance.

There are other roles for the manager in management development. Making sure that the staff people provide suitable alternatives, including internal programs, is important. The time invested by the manager need not be burdensome. One-half day a month per key subordinate should be adequate. It probably means that the manager will have to make a slight change in his or her own work habits to free up the necessary time.

Management time is much more valuable in management development than staff time. The real value of HR comes from design of systems and teaching employees and management alike how to perform their respective roles. Human resources' doing the manager's job does not result in an effective contribution. Teaching managers what their role is and insisting that they execute it effectively is real leadership.

Managers and employees alike, when working with effective HR functions in the future, will have to expect to be pushed into activities they find less than attractive. If they don't do what is needed, the HR function will probably turn into a dinosaur.

CONCLUSION

The HR function will turn into a dinosaur if it does any of the following on a regular basis:

Strives to be an equal player on the business team
Has control-oriented compensation programs like:
Position description
Thirty different pay grades with low ceilings

Uses input variables to determine pay grades

Works primarily on the supply side of human resources

Thinks it is a service function

Attempts to do the managers' work (e.g., in development) for them

Has a functional head who is just passing through

Accepts as employees failures from other functions

Doesn't make an extra effort to train and develop its members

Uses management by dominance as its underlying philosophy

No company should have HR functions that are dinosaurs, for if it does the business is likely to become extinct. The future world of work demands a much more enlightened attitude, philosophy, and role from HR so its contribution can become more valuable. The human resources issues in this volatile business climate may well be the most significant of all business challenges. If HR doesn't contribute it should be abolished. Line managers and employees have a right and a need to expect and get more. If the line is willing to make some changes in the way it approaches its work; and if HR gets its function to perform effectively, the future won't be easy, but it could be much more productive.

CHAPTER FIVE

Restructuring for Productivity

KIRBY WARREN

INTRODUCTION

Most call it downsizing; some, restructuring for productivity. A few have borrowed from the British—in deference to their far greater experience with euphemisms— and call it rationalization. Whatever the label, the actions involve major layoffs of managers and exempt professionals.

According to David Birch, a researcher at the Massachusetts Institute of Technology, employment at the nation's largest 500 companies dropped 2.2 million—to 14 million—between 1980 and 1985. As a result, people working for large companies, those defined as having at least 1000 employees, now represent an ever-decreasing share of the American workforce.

In New York, The Health Systems Agency has proposed eliminating 5000 of the 35,000 acute-care hospital beds over the next four years. As many as 20,000 jobs could be lost if the proposed plan takes effect. While major cutbacks, such as the publicized reductions in New York and California, received considerable attention in the press, downsizing in the public sector has been widespread. Private sector reductions range from major corporations facing serious troubles to strong, profitable companies that take action not through necessity but prudence.

Following the economic contraction of 1982, it is estimated that more than 100,000 steelworkers lost their jobs and, since that time, companies such as USX, LTV Corporation, and Bethlehem Steel have continued to streamline their operations in order to ensure their corporate survival.

In late 1986, the General Motors Corporation announced that it would close eight or nine domestic plants, resulting in the elimination of 29,000 jobs by 1990. Analysts estimate that

GM's long-run cost-cutting campaign will eventually require the elimination of 190,000 jobs worldwide.

AT&T continues to respond to the deregulated telecommunications industry. In December 1986, AT&T announced a $3.2 billion charge to fourth-quarter earnings that will finance future cost-cutting measures, including laying off 27,400 employees. Of these, 10,900 are management positions and 16,500 are nonmanagement jobs. After this round of job cuts has been completed, AT&T will have reduced its total employment to 290,000 from the 374,000 on the payroll as of January 1, 1984. MCI, AT&T's principal long-distance competitor, is also feeling the heat. MCI has recently announced plans to lay off 15 percent of its 16,000-member workforce, approximately 2300 jobs.

Not only those in serious, if not critical, condition have been forced to make such drastic cuts. Strong, profitable companies—many with significant growth records in recent years—have reduced their managerial and professional head counts significantly.

Exxon has revealed that it intends to reduce its U.S. workforce by approximately 15 percent. In mid-1986, 40,500 Exxon employees were given the option of accepting a severance package. Those over 50 and with at least 15 years of experience at Exxon were eligible for early retirement benefits. Others were given the option of accepting a lump-sum payment. Approximately 15 percent of those who were given the option of leaving, 6,200 employees, accepted the company's offer.

In the past five years, total employment at General Electric Company has shrunk by more than 100,000 to its current level of approximately 300,000. In early 1987, G.E. announced the elimination of an additional 3,400 jobs at turbine and aircraft engine plans across the country.

In mid-1986, CBS eliminated 600 positions from its broadcast division, representing 7 percent of that division's employees, and, later in 1986, IBM took a $250-million fourth quarter charge to cover the early retirement of 10,000 workers.

From 1946 until the early 1970s America's corporate leaders faced a combination of economic, competitive, technological, social, and demographic forces that made it difficult for them not to succeed. Some established corporations, through perseverance and creative neglect, managed to fail during this period, but it was indeed difficult.

In fact, both individual as well as collective failure during this period was at worst treated as a "learning experience" and those beyond resuscitation were often reincarnated in other organizations. Years of latent demand built from the worldwide depression of the 1930s through the devastation of World War II. While income in the United States increased during the war, shortages continued. The postwar period brought on the longest sustained boom in this century. In fact, the 1960s represent the only 10-year period (39 quarters) without a recession.

As the only major economic power to end World War II in better shape than it began, the United States with energy and decency sought to rebuild the world and profited greatly from the rebuilding. Unfortunately, during years of unparalleled opportunity and—by today's reckoning—benign, predictable competition, America's business leaders developed some very unfortunate habits.

What has caused these major reductions? Clearly, they cannot be explained solely by current economic conditions. Indeed, the roots of our current problems go back to the period immediately following World War II.

CAUSES

In 1946, after years of frugal effort to survive hard times and international war, corporate America suddenly faced a bonanza. Like individuals who had faced privation and fear and now saw great wealth ahead, corporations too went on a collective binge. Middle-aged, overweight Americans now seek the right diet plan and spend billions on exercise, weight reduction, and health clubs to try to get into shape. Corporate America likewise is struggling to find a way to shed its "flab" and regain the lean, lithe "body" that is necessary for today's competitive world. It is not surprising that for months the *Jane Fonda Workout* and Tom Peters' nostalgic look at excellence alternated at the top of the bestselling lists.[1]

To be sure, American industry was not led by fools. The executives who led us through the 1950s and 1960s were talented people who, like world-class surfers, required great agility and considerable balance and courage to stay in front of the wave. While vision was seldom rewarded, balance—staying on top—was. With some care, recovery from a wipe-out led to admiration and a chance to try again.

One anecdote reflects much of what happened, if not caused, our current preoccupation with corporate slimming and fitness programs. In 1959, Roger Blough, the chairman of the then undisputed leader of the steel industry, U.S. Steel, delivered a series of lectures at a leading university. At a dinner in his honor after one of the lectures, Crawford

---

[1]*Jane Fonda's Year of Fitness and Health, 1984.* NY: Simon & Schuster, 1983; T.J. Peters & R.H. Waterman, Jr., *In Search of Excellence.* NY: Harper & Row Publishers, 1982.

Greenewalt, then Chairman of duPont, poked a semicritical finger at Mr. Blough as only a peer can do. Greenewalt was a bit of a maverick in top business circles at the time. Having succeeded in rising to the top of the duPont corporation without being a duPont (he was but a son-in-law), he felt justified in criticizing the existing establishment.

"Roger," he asked after dinner, "What's going on in steel these days? While your sales and profits are at all-time highs I hear that the Germans and Japanese are not only taking back some foreign markets but even dropping some specialty steel tonnage here in America. I hope you aren't taking them too casually, Roger. What's going on?"

Blough's response (if not verbatim) was, "Well, Crawford, you must understand we weren't as lucky as the Germans and Japanese: We won the war! If they had bombed our mills in Pittsburgh, Gary, Youngstown, etc. and then provided us the capital for the latest technology, perhaps we would be able to do what they are doing."

After the audience's resounding applause died down, a professor (soon to be a former professor because of his undue emphasis on intemperate candor) remarked, "Sir, if the Germans and Japanese had bombed your mills, I don't think it would have made much difference unless management had been locked in them prior to the bombing. I truly believe it is your thinking, not your equipment, which is obsolete.

"The war has been over for 15 years. How much longer will it take you to write off obsolete equipment? Your overseas competitors have already replaced the technology we helped them with after the war. When will American industry begin to invest in the future rather than reap the benefits of the past?"

To be sure, such intemperance was impolite, if not overstated, but it got to the symptoms if not the causes of today's dilemma. So many of our industry leaders, like the Bloughs and Greenewalts, at best asked the right questions; at worst, accepted the wrong answers. These were not stupid men! They were bright, able, energetic, certainly; but hindsight shows their actions to have been unduly opportunistic, if not downright shortsighted.

Growth was taken as a given; staffing to meet growth needs essential. For some years after the war, finding enough "men" to staff managerial and professional positions was a major concern in America. Even those few women who had held such positions during the war left to resume more traditional roles and become the indispensable basis of the baby boom. Those women who did not choose to leave or sought an early return to professional employment were legally, if not openly, discriminated against. It is only since the late 1960s that this overt discrimination was abandoned.

Returning veterans came back to former jobs in fewer numbers than expected and often delayed entry into the managerial and professional workforce as they took advantage of the G.I. Bill to seek further education. High school graduates rejected professional "apprentice" positions and went on in larger numbers than ever to college.

Even when, by the early 1950s, these groups entered the workforce, the numbers of candidates for managerial and professional positions were fewer than needed. During this period of strong growth and high demand for talent, depression and World War II babies were the candidates. Given the extremely low birthrates in the United States from 1930 through 1945, this meant a supply far short of demand.

Personnel managers who had spent the prior 15 years sorting through applications looking for friends and relatives now had to leave the office and recruit. During the 1950s, demand for bright young high-potentials so outstripped supply that even an English major (the author) had six job offers at, for the time, very high starting salaries.

The signals from the top of the corporation were clear. "Get more. If you think we will need 20, hire 30. By the time we teach them something about the business, we will need them."

Leading companies faced high attrition rates as they often lost many in whom they invested several years of basic training to lesser competitors willing to cherry pick from the top corporations. While there may have been a search for excellence, when excellence is scarce, mediocrity takes on luster.

Booming profits and potential for growth, combined with a shortage of numbers, led to many shortsighted personnel practices. Fast-track candidates as well as older solid citizens were swept along by growth to positions for which they well might be unprepared and have difficulty managing. Deficiencies were hidden by growth. Jobs were shrunk to fit the talent available as "assistant to's" and other forms of managerial featherbedding became means of "temporarily" dealing with growth problems and limited human resources.

This is not to say that there were not many extremely able candidates driven by a competitive need to excel. There were many like this, but unfortunately not enough. Others in a slower growing, more demanding environment might have developed more fully, if not faced with open-ended opportunities early in their careers. The most able bloomed early; the least able got by. The best corporations succeeded in spite of talent shortages; the worst because of them.

By the mid-to-late 1970s, after at least 25 years of easy times, and several years of "rolling readjustment," unfit corporations suddenly found they were continuing to lose ground to leaner, more agile foreign and domestic competitors. Worse yet, they found they could not recover lost market share with size and bulk alone. The search for ways to create leaner, more lithe organizations began in earnest during this period.

THE EARLY EFFORTS AT CORPORATE SLIMMING

By the mid-1970s, the senior management of several corporations recognized what has now been somewhat unfortunately referred to as the pig-in-the-python syndrome. Whether interconnected or coincidental, the oil embargo and OPEC's actions to drive oil prices up arrived at about the same time as sluggish economic growth and the emergence of corporate Japan as a force to be reckoned with. From years of steady, real economic growth, the American economy moved toward stagflation at about the same time that years of hiring and preparation of young professionals caught up and passed the short-term demand for such talent. This pig-in-the-python syndrome led to a number of techniques to relieve the presence, if not alter basic emotions.

THE HIRING FREEZE

The IBM Corporation, after experiencing for several years not a *decline* in growth and profits but a decline in the *rate* of growth, concluded that it had to alter its hiring and development programs for managers and professionals. Twice in the late 1970s, IBM instituted what was virtually a year-long hiring freeze.

A senior IBM executive said, when interviewed by the author, "We simply have too many talented people working their way through middle management ranks and finding less challenge and opportunity for growth than they were accustomed to. While we seek to sort this out we must avoid compounding our problems by—for a short time—not bringing a new group of hard-chargers into entry-level jobs. It is bad enough that slower growth is impeding the movement of our middle managers up the organization; we don't want to add still more pressure below them at the same time."

Later, slow growth and increased domestic and foreign competition became recognized by other companies to be more than a rolling readjustment. Indeed, after more than a decade, even the most Pollyanna-ish corporations are now convinced that success, if not survival, demands getting *more* from *fewer* managers and professionals.

The need to reduce the number of managers and professionals is in many ways similar to reasons for reducing the ranks, but is compounded by several factors. Typically, managerial and professional positions are somewhat less structured, offering greater opportunity, indeed need, for allocating use of time and resources. Also ambition and opportunity for upward mobility typically serve as stronger motivators for these groups than within hourly ranks.

Overstaffing tends to blunt the need for and wisdom in setting priorities at precisely the time when a troubled organization needs more of both from its professionals. Similarly, lack of or slowed growth slows upward mobility and can lead the most able and ambitious to leave in search of greener pastures. Thus, firms most in need of able, ambitious professionals find them leaving—or at least less motivated and more frustrated if they stay.

The loss of prioritizing and motivation, if not the loss of top talent, is one of the three reasons for reductions in these ranks. The hope is that through painful pruning the best will have more opportunity and incentive to grow. A second reason is more obvious, namely reducing payroll costs in the light of lost sales and market share. A third reason stems from a desire to replace existing talent with different individuals.

Reductions brought about for the last two reasons may well see renewed hiring when sales and profits improve. It appears, however, that reductions designed to increase the incentive and opportunity to set wise but difficult priorities may be more permanent in nature. If indeed the organization can get not only "more" but "better" out of fewer, renewed growth is likely to see proportionately fewer new hires to replace those shed during earlier downsizings.

The earliest efforts to begin thinning managerial and professional ranks usually took the form of hiring freezes or "heavy frost." The next steps require actual removal of those employed.

Just as those at IBM recognized early, others have come to recognize that freezing or reducing new hires is at best a short-term source of only slight relief. Prolonged hiring freezes cut off much needed new ideas and energy, and ultimately produce large gaps in succession plans. While reducing temporarily at the base of the pyramid may be a start, sooner or later middle and senior layers must be reduced as well.

EARLY RETIREMENT (LOW PRESSURE)

The first steps in this direction typically involved seeking new ways to make early retirement more attractive. Given profit pressures, these early efforts to encourage more early retirees did not include new incentives. Travel posters in the cafeteria and write-ups in house organs on the joys of leisure villages were low-key means of thinning the ranks.

By and large, these programs failed. They attracted nowhere near enough to reduce management ranks significantly. Whether it was fear of double-digit inflation wiping out early retirement funds or concerns of a more psychological nature, few took the early retirement option. Compounding the problem, federal and state laws were moving toward extending, if not eliminating, forced retirement on the basis of age.

GOLDEN HANDSHAKES

In order to increase the numbers, some corporations began to offer, selectively, special arrangements for those willing to accept early retirement. Individuals were informed that should they "retire" within a relatively short period significant increments would be added to their retirement benefits. Implicit in some instances, explicit in others, was the belief that failure to accept the offer would be followed by dismissal.

While it is likely that some corporations continue this practice, they should recognize the risks. In a landmark case in 1973, a $750,000 award was made to the widow of an oil company manager who the court found was "forced" to retire. Many cases brought under the age discrimination law—including several class action suits by those *not* offered similar retirement incentives—have made this approach very risky.

GOLDEN WINDOWS

In order to avoid litigation on the basis of age discrimination while still making early retirement more attractive, more than 20 "window programs" have been created. These programs do not target *individuals* and seek their early retirement, but make the offer to significant *blocks* of employees.

For example, in one window program (so-called because the "window of opportunity" would remain open for but 30 days), the following conditions applied throughout the corporation: To be eligible, an employee needed to be more than 50 years of age with 25 years of service. All benefits would be vested and an additional two years of salary would be added to earned benefits.

Other window programs were limited to one division or one geographic location. Some offered more bonuses than others, but all sought to induce more people to retire without discriminating against those eligible as to who specifically should and who should not be made the offer.

Results of these programs are mixed. Some companies have reported that they still failed to generate a sufficient number of early retirements. One—duPont—indicated that a significantly larger number accepted their window than anticipated. All, however, shared in varying degrees a concern that they often "lost" some of their best people while others whom they hoped would retire clung to their positions in spite of offers they logically should have accepted.

Of all the early efforts at corporate slimming, window

programs appear to have been the most humane and probably the most successful. They are expensive, however, and uneven in that they reduce only the older population group. Further, because they lack the ability to discriminate legally among the best and worst of this age group, they may well lead to the loss of personnel with great value to the organization.

ACROSS-THE-BOARD REDUCTIONS

When the foregoing steps appeared too slow, too risky, too expensive, or insufficient, an alternative or next step was to institute across-the-board reductions.

In one large corporation, all divisions were required to submit plans within 30 days showing how they would bring about a reduction in headcount of at least 10 percent within three months. This reduction was to take place with (1) a commensurate reduction in total compensation, (2) no increase in consulting fees or subcontracting, (3) an expected 3 percent inflation rate, and (4) a sales growth goal of 8 percent. Meeting this 10 percent cut amounted to an 18 percent reduction of head count and a 21 percent drop in total compensation if the alternative had been to match real and inflated growth proportionally with head count and compensation increases.

Such arbitrary, across-the-board cuts ordered by top executives have several benefits. They are simple to understand and eliminate the need for rational justification, since there is none, and delegate the agonizing choice as to which departments should cut more, which less; and who stays, who goes.

When an organization is so bloated through years of bureaucratic neglect, such cuts do little real harm to the organization. While individuals may suffer and survivors may contribute to morale problems, typically there is little adverse effect on the firm. If enough surplus exists, it is not necessary to use a scalpel to remove, with surgical precision, excess flab. There is little danger of hitting muscle or crucial bone structure even when using an ax.

Such arbitrary and indiscriminate hacking, however, has many human costs. In some organizations, large numbers of young people are hurt since seniority is often the "best" criterion for effecting these cuts. This LIFO approach to slimming often creates victims whose only mistake was to join, or stay in, an overstaffed, underchallenged, or over-matched organization. In other organizations, we find FIFO the preferred approach. Flirting with age discrimination charges, several firms have cut senior, more highly placed personnel. Past experience indicates that over time these human costs may well have significant negative impact on organizational results.

Even more serious criticisms of the across-the-board approach apply when there is an uneven distribution of excess. When some divisions are bloated by years of good times and neglect while other, perhaps newer divisions, have remained leaner and more lithe, across-the-board cuts are aptly accused of leading to "survival of the fattest."

SELECTIVE REDUCTIONS

One would hope that senior managers would be sensitive to differences in divisional growth potential as well as their current condition, and make allowances for these differences. Unfortunately, our research has shown that this is frequently not the case. Interviews in 16 corporations and discussions with executives from another 21 companies indicate that frequently little effort is made to adjust reductions based on either past or projected performance. Whether they fail to make adjustments through lack of knowledge, lack of strength, or misguided sense of fairness to all is difficult to determine.

When rational adjustments *are* made, when some portions of an organization *are* asked to take large cuts and others smaller ones, or even are permitted increases in head count, an organization is usually well along in its slimming program.

Selective reductions occur least frequently early in the game when pessimism encourages sweeping cutbacks. Normally it is only after other techniques have been employed to whittle away large amounts of extra weight that the more selective thinning and firming programs begin. It is at this stage that most organizations should be ready in terms of size and attitudes to make the quantum leap and consider what, at present, for lack of a better term, we call "zero-based organizing." While it is entirely possible and probably desirable to consider this approach to creating leaner, more lithe organizations as a first step, most organizations seem to feel the need to begin by using one or more of the previously discussed means of thinning the ranks.

ZERO-BASED ORGANIZING

The concept of zero-based organizing, in fact, is based on two related notions. The first derives from zero-based budgeting efforts popularized (if not blown into fad proportions) in the 1970s. A zero-based budget started with blank sheets rather than last year's budget. The questions to be asked and answered were: "If we were starting from scratch, what would we do next year? What would those actions generate in revenues? What would they cost in period and capital outlays?"

The idea was to break away from extrapolations and start with the ideal set of actions, and from them determine benefits and costs. The difficulty was that, in preparing a budget for next year, those trying to break away from extrapolations were trapped by existing commitments or at least the perception that the current budget was laden with constraints on the next one. If an "ideal budget" *was* created, the sad conclusion frequently was, "That's where we would like to go all right, but you just can't get there from here."

The concept of zero-based organizing begins where zero-based budgeting does. It asks top management to break away from extrapolations from the existing organization. Start with a blank sheet of paper. Design the organization that represents the best size and form of departmentalization and delegation suited to strategic direction.

To succeed, however, it must depart from zero-based budgeting in two important ways. First, few organizations must have a new structure, a new organization, next year. Most can create a future structure that may take several years to reach. In theory, zero-based budgeters could have done the same with an "idealized budget" for, let us say, year five, allowing four years of work toward it. Unfortunately, few did. Instead, they were stopped by the notion that, "You just can't get there from here."

Russell Ackoff, one of the truly great minds applied to management practice, dealt with this seeming dilemma in his 1981 book, *Creating the Corporate Future*.[2] In short, what Ackoff argues is that, in creating an idealized future, how to get from here to there is the wrong question to answer. It can

[2]New York: John Wiley & Sons, Inc.

only lead to numerous psychological traps and blind spots that make the journey seem impossible. Ackoff argues that, in the context of creating a corporate strategy, the key question is how do we get from *there* to *here*.

The notion is far deeper than semantics. There are many problems in science as well as in philosophy that are far more difficult to solve through logical incrementalism than through reverse problem-solving. Ackoff seeks to create the desired future state on paper and then working backwards through successive approximations of the "ideal" state approaches the present from the future.

Zero-based organizing seeks to add this concept to creating the idealized organization. Start by thinking through the strategic direction of the business or sales force or the plant or the geographic territory. Then ask and answer, "If those are the strategies we believe will lead us to a sustainable competitive advantage, how, ideally, would we organize our resources to carry them out?"

This leads to a series of more specific questions and answers. Among the most crucial are:

1. What are the most important *tasks* that need to be carried out well in order to implement our plans?
2. How should these tasks be clustered? What key jobs would be created to do them?
3. Given needed linkages, coordination, and accountability, how much of what should be delegated to numerous doers and how much should be done by a few thinkers or planners?
4. How should these tasks/positions be departmentalized? Geography? Function? Customer? Product?
5. How should information technology be woven into

the organization design? When and to whom should it be a source of data? Alternatives? Recommendations? Decisions?

These and other questions lead to the creation of an idealized organization that constrains direction as to the size, shape, number, and networking. Assuming survival doesn't demand immediate transformation, the transition from current status through desired intermediate steps can take place over a two-to-three-year period. Taking more than three years to introduce a new structure probably dooms the change to failure. It is not only difficult to sustain commitment to change over a longer time span, but changing conditions may require major overhauls of strategy and structure before the organization has become accustomed to the first set of changes.

Once the organization that would be best suited to implement strategic direction has been conceived, Ackoff's logic must come into play. Do not look at the existing organization and ask how do we get from here to there. Using that as the next step will unavoidably increase the likelihood of the ideal structure being conceived with transition from the current one lurking in the corners of the designers' mind and unduly shaping their work.

In creating the ideal organization, the designers must do so knowing that their next task will be to look for approximations of this design that already exist somewhere outside the organization, if not in some part of their current corporation. Is there a plant organized like that? Has some other company tried a structure like this? must be the next questions. If no perfect or near-perfect examples can be found, studied, and used as models, then the next questions are,

"Well, what is almost done that way? What operates almost like that and is perhaps a little closer to our current approach?"

Gradually, the designers of a zero-based structure work their way back through a series of approximations of "perfection" toward the current structure, laying the "track" for progress from here to there in reverse.

Several corporations have already followed close approximations of this conceptual approach. One large and very successful organization, which has as its core business retailing, tackled the challenge in this manner. The chairman appointed a small but carefully selected group to the task of restructuring the company's retail operations. The group was asked, first, to review the company's assessment of retailing in the year 2001. What it would take to succeed in that environment was what they began considering. Based on their conclusions, they next asked how their company would compete in that world. This led to an update of their strategy plan for retailing and eventually to changes in other parts of the corporation's strategy for the next five years.

After consensus had been reached within the group and subsequently with the chairman, the same group was then asked to create the perfect organization to carry out this strategy.

"Don't tell me what we need next year," the chairman said. "Tell me what we would look like as an organization in five years if we are headed in that direction. Then we can start figuring out how to move from that future structure back to the present."

In the past three years more than a dozen major U.S. corporations have in whole or in part begun such a zero-based approach to restructuring. Several have started with a single division or business unit. Others seemed determined to tackle larger pieces. Still, too few have shown the leadership or determination to move beyond painful reductions toward a regime designed to provide continued progress. Without such thoughtful restructuring, there is very real potential for backsliding into the same condition as before.

CONCLUSIONS

For perhaps 25 years or longer, even the most successful U.S. corporations succeeded in large part as a result of extremely positive environmental conditions and leadership that was more opportunistic than visionary. From the mid-1940s through the early 1970s, economic, competitive, technological, and demographic forces produced a business environment for U.S. corporations that encouraged short-term opportunistic behavior.

During this period American businesses grew in size, profitability, and all too often became overstaffed and lacking in both the will to set longer term priorities and the agility to make rapid, successful short-term adjustments.

After some eight to 12 years of first denial and then progressive pain through downsizing and restructuring, much of corporate America has slimmed down and developed the resolve not only to read about excellence but truly pursue it. Organizations that have been through the most unpleasant part of this transition—having to reduce their staffing considerably—now face what may be the toughest but is certainly the most important phase of their sought-after renaissance.

Now they truly must seek to prioritize through strategic thinking. They must choose those markets, those products, services, and technologies for which sustainable competitive advantages can be realized. Then they must mold their structures, select and recruit new personnel, train and retrain their survivors to manage, to lead leaner, more lithe organizations. Restructuring now requires not only the careful thought suggested by zero-based organizing but commitments as well to creating planning, decision-making, measurement, reward, and penalty procedures that are appropriate to the restructured organization.

The "easy" years for American corporations are over. The tough years will continue. But the time has come to move from the ax to the scalpel in restructuring and to develop the systems and discipline to sustain the progress so painfully achieved.

CHAPTER SIX

Managers Through Time

DOUGLAS W. BRAY

An organization's managers are not a fixed quantity even when turnover is very low. Today's 45-year-old managers are not the same managers they were when they started in management at 25, and 25-year-old workers joining the organization today are not the same as the 25-year-old entrants of the previous generation. Individual and cultural changes are ongoing and determine the nature and attitudes of tomorrow's executives.

In this chapter the author will view the middle and senior managers of the future from two angles. One will be the managers themselves, their abilities, motivation, attitudes, and, by inference, their performance. The other will be a prediction of the problems executives will face in directing organizations composed of these managers.

THE AT&T STUDIES

The author has had a unique opportunity to study the managers of one large corporation, AT&T, for the past 30 years. The participants in the research have been studied more intensively than any other group of managers has ever been or is ever likely to be. The vast amount of data accumulated reveals much about the nature of managers, their careers, and how they change as time passes.

The AT&T research is made up of two parallel studies. The participants in the first, the Management Progress Study (MPS), started out as managers in the years from 1956 to 1960. Those in the second, the Management Continuity Study (MCS), joined the company from 1977 to 1982. This is not the place to detail the methodology of the research; it is available elsewhere.[1] It is necessary, however, to sketch the research design to give the reader a basis for understanding the findings that follow. The older study, MPS, will be described, since MCS, which parallels it, is still at an earlier stage.

The managers in MPS were exposed to a 3-day assessment center three times, usually in groups of 12. One assessment occurred at the start of the study, another eight years later, and the third 12 years later, that is, 20 years after the first. The assessments included interviews, paper-and-pencil tests, projective tests, and individual and group behavioral simulations. Abilities, motives, personality characteristics, attitudes, and values were evaluated. It was possible to assess later on only those who were still with the Bell System at years 8 and 20.

An extensive follow-up program took place in the years between the assessment centers. The participants were interviewed regularly, as were their bosses, and, of course, transfers and promotions were recorded. This follow-up has continued to the present. No information on individuals has ever been reported to the organization. Identification of records is solely by code number. Only one assessment has yet been done on the MCS, the more recent recruits. Follow-up procedures, however, have been substantially the same as in MPS.

The number of beginning managers included was 422 for MPS and 344 for MCS. About a third of those in MPS were non-college graduates who had advanced into man-

---

[1] A. Howard and D.W. Bray, *Managerial Lives in Transition: Advancing Age and Changing Times.* New York: Guilford Press, 1988.

agement from vocational jobs. The other two-thirds were college graduates hired in the expectation that they would show potential for advancement at least to middle management. Both groups consisted entirely of white males. In the 1950s, women and minorities were rarely considered as candidates for middle-management jobs.

There were no non-college participants in MCS. As in MPS, these young people with undergraduate or graduate degrees were hired on the assumption that they would advance up the managerial ladder. In other respects the sample differed, often noticeably. Times had changed. Half of the MCS participants were women and one-third were members of minority groups. In this chapter, comparisons with MPS will be limited to the white males. Extensive material on the women and minorities may be found elsewhere.[2]

The reader may well be inclined to question whether the findings from these studies are representative of managers in general or unique to AT&T. Ideally, parallel studies would have been conducted in other organizations, but nothing of similar scales had been attempted. The author and Ann Howard, last director of the studies at AT&T, were, however, able to throw some light on the extent to which AT&T's experience paralleled or differed from that of other large companies. They persuaded 10 organizations of substantial size to collect comparable data on their managers. Eight of the organizations were private enterprises, most of them quite large. One was an agency of the Federal government, the other of a state government.

The organizations in this Interorganizational Testing Study administered several of the paper-and-pencil tests

2Howard and Bray, 1988.

and questionnaires used in the AT&T research to a group of middle-aged as well as to a group of young managers matched with the AT&T groups. In all, about 400 of each age group were tested across the 10 organizations. The results were remarkably parallel to those in the AT&T sample. For example, young managers did not look forward to their future careers with much optimism. On an "Expectations Inventory," the young managers at AT&T scored at the 13th percentile while the outside sample scored at the 6th. In the 1950s, young managers were at the 51st percentile.

The highly similar pattern of results over all the instruments that were administered lent support to the author's conviction that the Bell System results could be safely generalized. After all, the telephone companies hired a significant percentage of all college graduates entering management each year. Before the break-up of the Bell System, anywhere from 2000 to 6000 new managers were hired annually. The author has also had many opportunities to present the AT&T results to human resources specialists in other companies. Nearly always, the reaction has been that similar results would have been obtained in their organizations.

Attention will now be turned to the young managers of the 1950s. Discussion will be limited to the college graduate segment of the MPS sample, since there are no non-college people in MCS, and the rise of non-college managers, even to the upper ranks of middle management, is becoming more and more of a rarity.

THE MPS RECRUITS

The typical college recruits of the 1950s entered the telephone business full of enthusiasm and ambition. They felt it would be a wonderful place to work. When they were asked to look ahead five years, 98 percent felt that more likely than not their jobs would be challenging with many opportunities to learn and do new things, while 99 percent expected their wives to be happy that they worked for the Bell System.

It was not at all unusual for these men to say that they planned to reach the vice-presidential level. They held to this assertion even when those conducting confidential interviews pointed out how few positions there were at that level. Almost two-thirds expected to be district managers within five years, a not impossible but highly ambitious goal.

Such ambitions were exaggerated but not basically inconsistent with the intentions of the college recruiting organization that had brought these young men into the business. The recruiters' goal had been to employ individuals who would remain with the company and reach at least the third (out of seven) level of management within 10 years or so. It was hoped that few would languish at one of the two lowest levels since there was assumed to be enough talent in the vocational ranks to fill such positions.

The MPS assessment center staffs who evaluated these recruits soon after employment threw cold water on this optimism. They saw no more than half of the group possessing the potential for the third or higher levels of management. Since ratings on individuals were confidential, this bad news caused the college recruiters more pain than it did the recruits.

Twenty years later only half of these young men were still employed by the Bell System. Although this is not a high attrition rate compared with many other corporations, the results did not bear out the rosy expectations of either the recruiters or the recruits. About half of those who left were asked to leave, while the rest departed voluntarily. Although the voluntary terminations had shown at the first assessment center about as much ability as those who stayed with Bell, they typically did not manifest high career potential. Although they were rated higher on motivation for advancement than either those who stayed or were asked to leave, they were rated lowest on primacy of work, occupational involvement, work standards, and flexibility.

At the 20-year mark, those who stayed with the company were distributed through six levels of management. No one had made it to the seventh level, president, by that time although that occurred shortly thereafter. Two others were vice-presidents, so that only three of the total group—less than 1 percent—reached the goal so many of them had projected when they first were hired.

Typically, the highest level achieved by these men was the third, which often carried the title of district manager. Some 46 percent were at that level. Since 20 percent were at second level and another 20 percent at the fourth, 86 percent of the group were above first level but below fifth level which was department head or assistant vice-president.

The original assessment center evaluations were strongly related to the management levels achieved 20 years later. Of the 63 men who had turned in the best performance at the assessment center, 43 percent reached the fourth level or higher. This compared to 20 percent of the other 74 men, better than a two-to-one ratio. (The reader is reminded that no one, not even the participants, was given any information on individual assessment performance.)

Since assessment performance was broadly predictive of progress in management, it was possible to analyze assessment center measures to discover the individual factors related to success. The assessment staff had made ratings of 26 dimensions, ratings based on three days of observation and testing. These were subjected to factor analysis and the factors correlated with achieved management level. Four factors emerged as the major personal factors in success. They were administrative skills, interpersonal skills (with an emphasis on leadership, general mental ability, and advancement motivation).

CHANGES OVER TIME

The fact that initial assessment evaluations accorded well with advancement over the two decades indicates that there was significant stability in the individual's characteristics. Nevertheless, as we followed the participants through their careers and assessed them on two successive occasions, we observed many important changes. For the typical participant, the rosy view of life as a manager had faded. Attitudes toward the company, although more favorable than unfavorable, were definitely critical. The drive for advancement, so intense at the outset, had for the most part waned. On a questionnaire addressing this motive, the average manager was now at the 8th percentile, compared to the 51st percentile 20 years earlier.

Advancement motivation is of such importance in the emergence of executives that the possible reasons for this sharp decline should be probed. We believe the most important reason was an adjustment to reality. As the men in the study progressed, the scarcity of openings at high levels became clear. They saw that the organizational form is more like a space needle perched on a broad base than a pyramid. Furthermore, some realized early that they did not have the ability or the dedication that a top job requires. These perceptions did not appear suddenly; the participants did not unexpectedly run into a stone wall. We found few who were deeply pained by stopping far short of the top. Most of them adjusted gradually and gracefully.

The story is more complicated, however, than these changes characteristic of the average manager. Changes in the attitudes and behavior of individuals varied by the management level that they attained. Those who advanced closer to the top developed differently from those who remained at the middle or lower levels. At year 20, those at levels 5 and 6 were the highest group in terms of motivation for achievement (to do a difficult job well), psychological investment in their job, and identification with management, to mention some of the key characteristics.

It is not surprising that those at the top were more involved in their work and had more favorable views of the company than those closer to the bottom. What was more surprising was that those who landed at levels 5 and 6 did not appear to be any more positively motivated (except for advancement) at the start of the study than the rest of the recruits. They differed little on motivation for achievement, for example, from those who finished at second level.

By the eighth year reassessment, those on their way to the top had spurted ahead in achievement motivation, leadership motivation, job involvement, and other motives, and had the highest scores. Those who were to finish their careers at levels 1 or 2, on the other hand, had declined in job involvement right from the start. Those who were to reach third level showed no change.

These findings have led the author to postulate on "formative response" to early experience in management.[3] Some respond with enthusiasm to the challenges of manag-

---

[3]D.W. Bray. "Assessment Centers for Research and Application." Psi Chi Distinguished Lecture, meeting of the American Psychological Association, Toronto, Canada, 1984.

ing while others turn off when the realities of organizational life directly impinge upon them. This is one reason that organizations should pay close attention to early job assignments and the nature of early supervision. Commitment can be lost quickly.

People do not rise to the top because of motivation alone. Ability counts! How did those who moved ahead the furthest stand in general mental ability, administrative skills, and interpersonal skills—areas that we found to be the most important in progressing in management? When assessed at year 8, the high achievers were several notches above those at the lower levels on each of these three areas. Their advantage in administrative and interpersonal skills was large. In general mental ability, however, they were only slightly higher than those who would reach fourth level, although they were clearly higher than those who failed to make that level.

At the first assessment, 20 years earlier, these high-level managers had already been in the top group in mental ability, but the story behind the two management skill areas is more complex. At original assessment the eventual high-level participants did not differ much in interpersonal skills from those who would reach levels three and four, and they showed exactly the same level of skill eight years later. But they were clearly superior to the rest, since the scores for all other groups had dropped!

Such a phenomenon deserves comment. It is difficult to think of individuals losing interpersonal skills. It would seem that once a person had attained a level of such skill he or she would always have it. The explanation for the loss of skill is probably motivational. Our data show that as the participants grew older, they became more prone to feelings of hostility and more eager for independence. They came to care less about behaving smoothly in group situations. The highest level men, having done well, didn't change their behavior. There was, moreover, a strong correlation between the size of the decline in the interpersonal skill score and behavior and level of achievement. The groups at the bottom showed the largest decline.

The situation was again different in the case of administrative skills. At the first assessment those who would go furthest were not outstanding. They did no better than those who would reach only the fourth, third or even the second level. But the next eight years really made a difference! The most successful were the only group to improve, and they left the rest far behind. Apparently the rising motivation of the most successful group, supported as they were by good mental ability, resulted in a great deal of learning.

Some of the managers in the MPS have retired, and others are considering doing so. Many will, of course, stay for a while, and some might even hold on until the year 2000. But it is clear that few, if any, will become tomorrow's executives. That role will be limited to those who have entered business more recently. In the telephone companies, a sample of tomorrow's executives make up the Management Continuity Study.

THE NEW MANAGERS

The MCS recruits joined the telephone companies from 1977 to 1982. They presented a quite different picture from their counterparts 20 years earlier. They were not nearly as full of enthusiasm and ambition. On a scale measuring motivation for advancement, they averaged the 21st percentile compared to the 51st for the MPS men at the start of their careers. Most of the newcomers aimed not at vice-presidency but at the fourth level of management.

Neither were those in MCS as motivated to lead. Here the typical recruit was at the 34th percentile as compared to his counterpart in MPS at the 49th percentile. Thus two important motives relied on for decades to drive perform- ance and the climb to high places have become greatly weakened. It is important to keep in mind that these results are averages. They do not imply that none of the young managers is motivated to lead and to move upward toward the top. It means, rather, that there are fewer with strong ambitions.

The new recruits were, in addition, not as optimistic about the life of a manager or the company that employed them. Less than a majority were sure that their job, five years down the road, would be challenging and that opportuni- ties for promotion would be greater than elsewhere. Only 19 percent strongly rejected the statement "I feel that the company resists new ideas and experimentation." Less than 20 percent felt sure that significant conflict between job and family could be avoided. Some stated frankly that they weren't at all confident that a career in management was right for them, but that they felt they should give it a try.

The new group was comparable in overall management ability to the beginning MPS group. There was no signifi- cant difference between the two groups in administrative skills, but there were differences in the other two ability areas. The new recruits scored significantly higher in gen- eral mental ability, but lower in interpersonal skills. Since this last skill was rated on the basis of performance in a group exercise, it may be that their lesser motivation to lead holds the explanation.

What did these new managers want from work? They were, it turned out, just as interested in good pay as the older men. They were also just as interested in challenging work that would make use of their abilities. In addition, they had a strong desire to do a quality job. Thus they had much to build on, but it seemed certain that they would become very impatient if their needs were not quickly satisfied.

At the moment we can only hypothesize about the changes that will take place in the motives and attitudes of these new managers as they move through their early careers. The research plan calls for the reassessment of these participants within the next two years, which would provide the answers. However, the divestiture of the telephone companies from AT&T and the changes within AT&T itself may alter this plan. For the moment, we can only speculate.

If we assume that the changes will parallel those for the Management Progress Study, we can make predictions about how the MCS group will look eight to 10 years into their careers. In motivation for advancement, the average MPS participant dropped from the 51st percentile to the 28th at year 8 and to the 8th percentile at year 20. MCS started off at the 21st. We can expect the drive to advance to be at a very low ebb in the 1990s.

As time went by, the attitudes of the average MPS manager toward the company became less and less favorable, although they never became outrightly unfavorable. We have seen, however, that the MCS group began with much more negative attitudes. The intensification of such views would present a major morale problem.

That such a trend is indeed possible was indicated by a retesting that we were able to undertake with part of the MCS sample at year 4. This was done to check on the hypothesis that having started out with less favorable expectations, the MCS group might not decline as sharply as had the MPS. This did not turn out to be true; the MCS ratings declined just as steeply even though their initial standing was well below the MPS.

The MPS men rose significantly in motivation for

achievement particularly during the early years. Since the MCS began at the same level as MPS, it would appear that management can continue to count on a good level of this motivation in the future. The problem will be whether this can be capitalized on in light of the other less favorable motives.

As far as abilities are concerned, mental ability will not be in short supply since the MCS group was clearly superior to MPS; and mental ability does not decline with age, except for the very old. In fact, the verbal aspect of intelligence increases with age.

Interpersonal skills possessed, or at least displayed, may be expected to decline sharply for the average manager. The predicted deterioration of attitudes toward the organization, with concomitant hostility, would make this area even more hazardous.

Administrative skills will not change much for the average manager. It is rather surprising that experience does not make for improvement. In the absence of interventions, such as effective coaching or training, managers seem to keep doing things in their own accustomed way.

We saw in MPS that those who reached executive levels developed quite differently from other groups. Their motivation not only did not decline, it increased. Interpersonal skills remained intact, and administrative skills improved greatly. Attitudes toward work and toward the organization were strongly favorable.

It may be that even in the face of the weak motivation and negative attitudes of the average MCS recruit, a sufficient number of the new managers will develop much as did the MPS executives. After all, only 11 percent of those who stayed with the telephone company reached this level, which is only 5-1/2 percent of all those who were originally employed. Yet there are signs that many organizations today do not provide a climate fostering such development.

ORGANIZATIONAL TRENDS

Thus far we have discussed the characteristics of managers and how these characteristics change over the course of their careers. We have ignored the corporation, treating it implicitly as a maze through which managers and would-be managers find their way according to their abilities and motivation. Yet organizations change through time in ways that alter the maze. More importantly, individual development is strongly affected, for better or worse, by the changing nature of the organization.

Until recently organizational change was not a matter of general concern. Giants such as General Motors and AT&T moved along through the years, their bureaucracies purring smoothly. They always had been there and they always would be there. A manager who wasn't manifestly incompetent or dishonest was assured a job for life.

How the scene has changed! Foreign competition, technological innovation, governmental intervention, takeovers, and divestitures have played havoc with the placid environment of the American corporation. The lean-and-mean look has become fashionable. Layers of management have been erased, functions have been eliminated, managers have been coaxed or pushed into early retirement, and others have been summarily dismissed.

In spite of these striking trends, some of the young people starting in management today will stay with their original employer. How will they develop under these new circumstances? We have seen that even in a stable organization attitudes degenerated, feelings of hostility increased, and interpersonal behavior became less effective. Such negative developments must be expected to be much worse in the turbulent and insecure climate that now prevails.

It is noteworthy that these profound changes in the nature of organizational life are taking place just when many young managers show weak motivation for corporate life, and "show-me" attitudes are strong even before they get started. How many of the survivors of downsizing and personnel purges are going to tell young managers that they have it all wrong? It seems inevitable that motivation and commitment will become even worse with time, and that those who do not leave will turn off.

The unsympathetic observer might ask how much it will matter if they do turn off. Presumably they will have to do their job or be fired. But what is a job? Business today recognizes that it is more than just performing the operations for which one is responsible. Participative management, a passion for excellence, the quality of work life, affirmative action, and multiculturalism are some of the important goals that organizations now stress. Turned-off managers may turn the production cranks, but it will prove impossible to enlist them in the struggle for corporate survival.

Given the likely failures in the positive growth for managers who stay with the same company, it is worrisome to realize that college graduates or MBAs starting with a company today can no longer look forward confidently to spending their entire career with their initial employer, even if they perform well. They must expect to change employers several times. As a colleague put it, a career may become a series of superficial affairs rather than a life-long love match. This means that managers will have to think about building a career involving job-hopping. Their resumes had better always be in the hands of effective headhunters.

Possibly new ways will emerge. Managers, no longer expecting a life-long career, may demand contracts. The negotiations of baseball managers with the team owners come to mind. Talented managers will see themselves more as mobile professionals than as loyal officers dedicated to one employer. They may become corporate mercenaries.

The average undistinguished middle manager may not fare so well. There may be a continuing market for his or her skills so that long periods of unemployment will not be a high risk. But the likelihood of having to move on after being employed for a while may prevent satisfaction with one's work. And since work satisfaction is an important part of life, life itself may be less satisfying.

Executives now face a host of problems in pursuing the goals of efficient production of quality products, marketing, and profit making. No doubt they could compile quite a list of problems. One suspects, however, that the managerial workforce, if mentioned at all, would be restricted to the matter of numbers. Many see the problem as getting rid of the fat in management. There are many more problems than that!

Fat or lean, middle and lower-level managers of the future may be a recalcitrant bunch. The strong tendency of managers to lose motivation as they grow older will be compounded by the initially weak motivation of the current generation of new managers. Both of these trends will be intensified if organizations are seen as cold and uncommitted to their managers as they pursue cost containment and rigorous efficiency. Executives may find that corporate goals are elusive when the only ones interested in playing hard are they themselves.

History has moved along. Neither employers nor employees are what they used to be. Things were never Uto-pian, but now Utopia seems much farther away. Perhaps some future executives will make things better.

CHAPTER SEVEN

Executives in Four Fields

JOHN T. DUNLOP

The four fields in this assigned topic are private business, labor organizations, government agencies, and academic administration apart from the professoriate. The configuration is based on the editor's conviction that my experience shows scars from each of these fields. But these areas often involve considerable overlap: Academic administration may be private or governmental and may include responsibility for residential operations, hospital management, and complex scientific facilities; business executives may range from trade associations and nonprofit organizations through research bodies to general managers of profit centers; and government executives may encompass a vast scope from public business enterprises, such as the postal service, utilities, and defense installations, to the broad policy-making and diverse administrative agencies of Federal, state, and local governments. To recognize the full continuum and common elements of executive activity in each of these fields does not preclude attention to separate modal types provided the complexities of reality are not ignored.

The title suggests administrative, executive, and leadership roles *within* organizations. The attention is not focused on the isolated individual who may have significant impact on the larger society, despite an organizational home, as with Nobel laureates in the sciences, potential saints and prophets, great writers of fiction, visionary political leaders, and the like. We are dealing with men and women who make their contribution and achieve their rewards *through* organizations in these four fields.

The observations that follow are not the product of specific research as that activity is understood currently in the social sciences; they grow out of operating experience, contacts with students in all four fields over many years, and the research and reflections of others. They have little if anything to do with the discipline of economics that today has little to say about the behavior of organizations and their leadership. A brief bibliography is appended that includes works that, in my view, are insightful in the four fields and in their interactions. A list of selected biographies would also provide further understanding.

The observations that follow are confined to the United States. They do not necessarily apply to other countries. In France the role of the *grandes écoles* such as Normale and Polytechnique or the University of Tokyo in Japan train a business and government leadership that has no counterpart here. The presidency of the American college and university is unique since in continental Europe and Latin America the rector is confined within a narrow corridor between the power of the faculty guild and a government ministry in charge. In the Soviet Union the role of the party in the recruitment and designation of leadership in organizations are alien by our standards.

This chapter is divided into the following sections: Common Elements Among Executives in Four Fields; Distinctive Elements Among Executives in Four Fields; Changing Characteristics of Executives in Four Fields; and Some Degree of Convergence.

COMMON ELEMENTS AMONG EXECUTIVES IN FOUR FIELDS

There appear to be certain common elements in executive performance among these fields, although the significance and weight attached to each varies widely among and within each. While diverse conceptual schemes and terms have been used by scholars, the central ideas are relatively simple and straightforward.

1. Environmental Analysis

The executives need to understand and articulate the environment within which the organization operates and the likely changes in that milieu in the short and longer periods ahead. At times the exterior world of the organization, and its major changes, may be described in extended statistical terms citing demography, including educational levels, language, regional and age distribution, the technological factors, budgetary outlook, and the domestic and international competitive developments impinging on the institution. In most large-scale organizations such formal environmental analysis has come to be the starting point of strategic planning. At other times in other fields the perception of environmental change is little more than the intuitive sensitivities of the leadership scanning the horizon with a finger up to test the wind and steering by the seat of the pants. Such archaic methods have on occasion proven highly successful. Whatever the approach, executives across these four fields, irrespective of the differing situations that they faced, have the responsibility and need of understanding the changing external environment and its impact on the organization.

2. Setting Goals and Priorities

The articulation of specific objectives and the establishment of priorities for an organization are central features of the executive common to these four organizations and, indeed, to almost any executive worthy of the name. But the function is not simple. There may be competing objectives, and the achievement of one goal may diminish the possibility of accomplishing another. Resources of all kinds are limited, including the time and energy of the executive. Moreover, the specification of goals and priorities may involve keen internal conflict among factions and elements of the organization. The maintenance of a measure of internal cohesion and morale is vital to the mobilization of organizational effort and achievement of defined goals. All this is a fine art, for any organization trying to go several different ways at once or consumed in intensive conflict is not likely to go far.

3. Selection and Development of People

The central importance of human resources is common to these four organizations. They depend crucially on the performance of their people. But people do not come as ready-made pegs to fit into fixed organizational holes. They need to be selected and recruited, trained, educated, moved about, promoted, motivated, compensated, rewarded, and even disciplined. The organization may even need to be reshaped, on occasion, to accommodate particular individuals and talents. The selection and development of people is at the center of the functions of the executive and the performance of the organization.

4. Shaping the Structure of the Organization

The molding and reshaping of the organization, in the light of the changing environment, the specified short-term and longer term goals and priorities, and the development of its people is no less a distinctive function of the executive in these fields. The levels of the management hierarchy, the lines of reporting formally and informally, the controls over money flows, the relations with the press and media, relations to governments, and the interactions with other exterior groups are all reflective of the arrangement or structure of an organization. The executive is responsible for the contours and structure of the organization, although for a period of time some features may be entirely intractable.

5. Negotiating Skills

In dealing with internal organizational problems as well as external entities and constituencies, the skills of negotiation and consensus building are indispensible. Executives are seldom able to achieve their objectives by simple fiat. Making allowance for differences in personal style, an organization seldom operates by the lines of formal authority, and external relations are seldom determined solely by impersonal markets or economic power.

6. Generating and Introducing Innovation

Change is typically mandated by different goals of the organization or the emerging environment; executives are thus peculiarly concerned with the development and introduction of innovation. Change is inevitably a disturbance to an organization, or to some of its members, and inertia and resistance may thwart desired innovation or extract too high a cost in friction and conflict. The art of planning and introducing organizational change is a key feature of the job of the executive, more important in some organizations and at some periods than in others.

DISTINCTIVE ELEMENTS AMONG
EXECUTIVES IN FOUR FIELDS

Although the characteristics of executives in these fields in an important sense constitute an overlapping continuum, as noted at the outset, it is also instructive to identify the distinctive elements that characterize executives in these four fields, treating each field as an "ideal type." Although a modest degree of abstraction is necessarily involved, hopefully additional insights and generality can be achieved that are summarized in Table 1 at the end of this section.

1. Measures of Performance

The performance of the business executive is measured by the bottom line, short term or longer run, or by more sophisticated indicators of value creation in a market. Government executives are ultimately adjudged by the bottom line of votes and by more diffuse judgments of programmatic records with few common denominators. The performance of academic executives tends to be related to the diffuse judgments and standards of the constituencies of students, faculty, and alumni. The performance of labor leaders is reflected in the quality of the collective bargaining agreements they negotiate and the internal governance of the union expressed in votes of members or delegates at the next election in a one-party government. These are quite different substantive tests in quite different organizational settings.

2. Consideration of Efficiency and Equity

The market subjects business executives to the prime considerations of profits, productivity, and market performance while political executives—including senior civil servants—are far more concerned with relative equity and the appearance of fairness. Despite the rhetoric, to reshape a government to conform to an executive's view of efficiency is inhibited by the checks of the legislative and judicial branches. In the dimension of efficiency–equity, the academic executive confronts still different tests of efficiency—such as academic distinction and student application—that cannot be ignored; but in general the trade-off leans toward custom and equity. Only extreme circumstances are likely to lead, for instance, to the closing of a department or a school on grounds of efficiency, and a layoff of tenured faculty on efficiency grounds is virtually precluded. In labor organizations the internal politics and the public law—the duty of fair representation—place the emphasis on equity at the far end of the efficiency–equity spectrum.

3. Command and Persuasion

The ideal type of the business executive achieves internal results—organizational structure, delegation, policy, and administration—by command or control. Orders are issued, reports are received, and compliance is achieved or discipline dispensed as in a military-type organization. The government executive is far more indirect, probing the reactions of the wide array of constituencies in and out of government typically affected and the possible reactions of other branches of government, and paying great attention to the packaging and timing of proposals; in short, bowing to the arts of persuasion rather than to the issuance of orders. The academic executive confronts endless consultation and debate in a milieu in which changing one's mind may be regarded as a virtue and in which various constituencies may assert overlapping claims of superiority. Union executives exert considerable control over internal administrative matters, but they typically require major assent of membership on collective bargaining agreements and politically sensitive activities. Taking actions the executive is convinced are necessary for the organization—that are unpopular—often tests to the limits the power of persuasion or occasionally the willingness to use up power.

4. Private or Public Processes

The processes of internal business decisions take place essentially in private and are made public or their consequences become evident at the discretion of the enterprise, although the timing of some reports may be dictated by government regulation. Indeed, there may even be government penalties for acting on "insider information." In marked contrast, public executives, particularly in politically sensitive positions, are typically engaged in an exchange with press and the media at each step of the decision-making process. The news leak is well understood to be often a means of internal government conflict rather than a result of assiduous investigation by the news media. As Secretary George P. Shultz said, "We should recognize what life is like in Washington. The Canadian ambassador coined the phrase, 'It's never over.' Nothing ever gets settled in this town. It's not like running a company or even a university. It's a seething debating society in which the debate never stops, in which people never give up, including me."[1] Academic executives usually have some of the freedom of

[1]*New York Times*, December 9, 1986, p. A-14.

business decisionmakers save that student newspapers often hound the process, and academic participants are not constrained to express their views on pending matters as are members of management. Labor organization processes are seldom reported in the public press, while the internal news organs are controlled by the leaders. Informal lines of internal communication often provide effective exchange of information.

5. Personnel Constraints

The business executive has rather wide discretion in decisions on selecting from within or drawing from outside the management organization, on assigning and compensating members of the organization. There are, of course, constraints established in public law such as in race, sex, and age discrimination. Any related reform or realignment of the management structure is no less pliable. The government executive, in contrast, faces severe constraints either by civil service rules or by requirements for political appointment. Recruitment procedures constrict choice; transfer and promotions are regulated; compensation is strictly confined; and discipline and discharge are subjected to complex and slow-moving procedures and appeals. I once compared the procedures of the government executive to the management of a glacier. The management of the professoriate in the academic world is no less constrained in process than the civil service; but personnel constraints applicable to executives outside the professoriate in private educational institutions are relatively unrestrained, while in public institutions they are akin to higher levels of the civil service and the political processes. Labor union executives have relative freedom of appointment to staff save for the traditions of drawing from the ranks for line positions and as restricted by political considerations and assignment of certain posts to election results, as in the case of organizers or district directors in some unions.

6. Length of Service

This dimension of an organization affects the time horizon of an executive, as well as the turnover of executives, and may influence the stability of the organization. Top executives in business tend to have a considerable length of service, although they may be removed by the board of directors or top management. In recent years the merger and takeover developments have placed these positions in some jeopardy, although many positions have been protected by various types of parachutes. The government executive is constrained by the calendar of elections, which brings changes not only among political appointees, but rearrangements that affect the status of senior civil servants. This environment reinforces a short-term horizon. Academic executives tend to serve for terms also without specification, although the late 1960s and 1970s saw a reduction in length of service. Elected officers of national unions tend to serve for specified terms of four or five years that tend to be renewed for relatively long periods, although there is much more turnover among elected local officials.

The first section identified six elements common to the function of executives in all fields and particularly these four fields: business, government, academia and labor organizations. We then identified six features of the role of executives in ideal types of these four fields that reflect significant differences among the constructs of these fields. Table 1 summarizes these contrasts.

TABLE 1
Contrasts Among Four Fields

Element	Business	Government	Academic	Union
1. Measures of performance	Profits or value creation	Votes, programs	Judgment of students, faculty, and alumni	Votes of members
2. Efficiency and equity	Market performance efficiency	Largely equity	Academic efficiency bows to equity and custom	Largely internal equity
3. Command and persuasion	Command and control	Extensive persuasion first	Extensive and lengthy consultation	Administrative command and political notification on policy
4. Private or public processes	Private until released	Public at each step	Largely private with periodic exposure	Internal, officially controlled with informal lines
5. Personal constraints	Large degrees of management freedom	Strict civil service restraints and political processes	Academic strict processes	Relative freedom except as limited by political and election processes
6. Length of service and time perspective	Relatively long term in most cases but with increasing insecurity	Limited by short-term election results	Relatively unconstrained although reduced in 1960s and 1970s	Renewed specified terms at national levels

CHANGING CHARACTERISTICS OF EXECUTIVES IN FOUR FIELDS

Executives have been changing in these fields in part on account of changes in their environment, in part because of developments in their organizations; and some of the change is attributable to the qualities of the executives, although it is not possible to assign magnitudes to these components of change.

1. Increasing Education Level of Executives

The general level of education in the country, and the percentage with college degrees and professional training, continues to increase, affecting each generation of executives. Moreover, the past quarter century has seen a very rapid expansion in the extent of "executive education"— short courses, ordinarily at universities, designed for practicing executives to meet with similar executives from other organizations for periods of from four to 12 weeks to consider issues confronting decisionmakers portrayed in "cases," to be instructed on recent developments and new techniques, and to reflect on organizational processes and goals. These programs have become widespread for executives drawn from business and government and are probably less extensive for academic and trade union executives. The Harvard Business School began its Advanced Management Program after World War II, a variety of programs in the School of Government date from the 1970s; programs for higher education executives date from the 1960s, and the Trade Union Program was established in 1942.

But it is easy to exaggerate the influence of formal education in the development of executives. "Since fewer than 20 percent of the chief executive officers of large corporations have business school degrees (although the figure is rising), there is even a nagging possibility that formal training is unnecessary for effective management."[2] Given the extraordinary range of work performed by Federal government employees,[3] it is not surprising that throughout the service many executives are not well trained. Academic executives in the major positions are seldom selected for their managerial skills or executive training, and labor union leaders are elected in a process that is not likely to stress executive skills either.

2. Different Routes to the Top

The ladders of promotion and the "ports of entry" to executive positions in these organizations are a matter of interest, as well as whether there have been significant changes in these routes to executive posts. In business organizations, internal promotion is the most common route to general managerial and executive posts. But the transfer from other organizations, particularly other businesses, has become more common in recent years by the willingness of enterprises to look outside combined with the growth of personnel recruitment firms, or headhunters, as a serious business undertaking as well as by the merger and takeover processes that reshuffle executives.

In government, the civil service provides various,

[2]Derek C. Bok and John T. Dunlop, *Labor and the American Community,* New York, Simon and Schuster, 1970, p. 104.

[3]Howard Rosen, *Servants of the People, The Uncertain Future of the Federal Civil Service,* Salt Lake City, Olympus Publishing Company, 1985, pp. 13–29.

though limited, points of entry and ladders of promotion. That system has not reflected major changes in recent years despite the creation of the senior civil service and the effort to encourage greater mobility. The political appointees constitute the other entry and structure of advancement for executives, and here again there appears to have been little change, although the proportion of posts that are political appointees has been much increased in recent years.

Most academic executives, as might be expected, come directly from academic or administrative life on a college campus. As high as 85 percent of presidents come from this source, and half of the remainder have had experience in academic life as a faculty member or administrator. "This route of access is natural because academic institutions have their own ways of doing things and it is important to be acquainted intimately with them."[4] Most academic presidents (80 percent), however, come directly from outside the institution of which they become chief executive. Length of service has declined from 10–12 years prior to the mid-1960s, to seven years currently.

National union executives are selected almost without exception from among their members and ordinarily by the well defined ladder consisting of business manager of a local union, a representative for the national union, a vice-president of the national union, and the top office. There may, of course, be some variation in the ladder, including another local union office, an officer of a district council, joint board, or some other intermediate body. Only extremely rarely does an outsider, a non-rank-and-file member, reach the top rank through a professional staff role. As

[4]Clark Kerr and Marian L. Gade, *The Many Lives of American Presidents, Time, Place and Character*, Washington, D.C., Association of Governing Boards of Universities and Colleges, 1986, pp. 18–19.

C. Wright Mills expressed the point in 1948, "The union world is a world of political machines; the labor leader is a machine politician."[5] Only a deadlock between communist and noncommunist factions brought Ralph Helstein, the union's lawyer, as a compromise candidate to the presidency of the Packinghouse Workers after World War I. Unlike some unions in other countries, political leaders, newspaper editors, or leaders of social movements are not likely to enter the leadership of American labor unions. The public regulation of the election process in our unions by the Labor-Management Reporting and Disclosure Act of 1959 (Title IV) has not made significant changes in ports of entry or internal ladders to executive posts.

3. The Leader–Follower Relationship

The relationship between executives (leaders) and lower level officers of the organization and the main body of constituents is vital to the performance of the organization and to the way it, and its executives, may have changed over a period of years. There are, of course, marked differences generally between the interactions of business executives and stockholders; government executives and legislative bodies and voters; academic executives and the constituents of students, faculty, and alumni or legislators; and union executives and members; and each setting is surrounded by internal rivalries or opposition and by the relevant press and media. Moreover, the relationships also vary according to whether the organization is in a period of calm or crisis, prosperity or recession, or in rapid growth or stagnation.

[5]C. Wright Mills, *The New Men of Power, America's Labor Leaders,* New York, Harcourt Brace & Company, 1948, p. 5.

"One generalization that is supported by research and experience is that effective two-way communication is essential to the proper functioning of the leader-follower relationship."[6] It needs to be borne in mind that few organizations or constituencies are homogenous and that executives are constantly at work in two-way processes, in some organizations more than others, to develop a full consensus or a working consent to policies and administration. Line executives in business have historically been less involved in this process since it was deemed less necessary, although recent years have seen vastly more attention to stockholder communications and the courting of stock analysts.

Executives in all four fields in recent years have been confronted with new problems that probably require new methods in their relationships to lower level officials and constituencies. The stockholders, electorates, and memberships have become better educated and more widely read; and much more information or disinformation is available. The television media, which cannot be fully influenced, have direct access to the constituency. As a consequence, these constituencies have become in many cases more independent and more divided or less homogenous in their willingness to follow the executive blindly. Such constituents are likewise more vulnerable to external as well as internal opposition. The executives in many cases have been compelled to devote much more time and energy to the reinforcement of the organization and to systematic discourse and education of lower levels of the organization and constituents. "A loyal constituency is won when people, consciously or unconsciously, judge the leader to be capable of solving their problems and meeting their needs, when the

[6]John W. Gardner, *Leadership Papers*: "The Heart of the Matter, Leader-Constituent Interaction," p. 9.

leader is seen as symbolizing their norms, and then their image of the leader (whether or not it corresponds with reality) is congruent with their inner environment of myth and legend."[7]

The tasks of executives are often made more difficult by these modern conditions, particularly when rapid and major changes are dictated by the environmental analysis and the goals of the organization. The constituencies are more independent, more divided, less willing to accept the dictates of the executive, and more apt to mount demonstrations and opposition.

New executive methods and styles are generated and new types of executives are called. Business executives need to be at home in dealing with government officials, legislators, and the media as well as with finance, production, and marketing. Government executives require even more developed skills of accommodation and sensitivity to constituencies. "Academic executives are many-faced, in the sense that they must face in many directions at once while contriving to turn one's back on no important group. They are mostly mediators."[8] Union executives need to accommodate their membership, employers with whom their organization deals, governmental agencies, and the public. The task of generating organizational momentum toward cherished goals is constrained by managing diverse internal elements and external constituencies. There is little room between destructive organizational conflict and immobility in a rapidly changing environment.

[7]Gardner, p. 11.

[8]Clark Kerr, *The Uses of the University*, Cambridge, Harvard University Press, 1963, p. 36.

4. The Difference in Generations of Executives

The generational contrasts between those who grew up with experience in the Great Depression and World War II and those who reached maturity in the 1970s and 1980s are said to have significant impacts on all of these four fields, both on the executives and on their constituencies. These age contrasts, if they persist, may affect in significant ways the performance of executives and the methods they use to achieve organizational goals.

Surveys suggest that these generational contrasts are not influenced by ethnic background, occupation or sector of the economy.

"The older generation, products of the World-War-II era, accept authority. The younger generation, having grown up during Vietnam, do not trust authority.

"The older generation see work as a duty, an instrument through which they can support themselves and their families. The younger generation believe work should be fun, a social occasion.

"The older generation believe experience is the necessary road to promotion, and are willing to spend time in 'apprenticeship.' The younger generation see no reason to wait, believing people should advance just as quickly as their competence permits.

"The older generation believe in tact. The younger generation demand honesty and candor—to them, tact is seen as evasion of the issues.

"The older generation believe that fairness is achieved by treating everyone the same. The younger generation believe that fairness requires that individuals should be allowed to be different."[9]

The characteristics of the younger generation suggest the need for "a better fit between a company and the individuals who compose it; we need a lively, open, risk-taking view of the world in corporations today."[10]

The post-war baby boom was such a large cohort in the population as it moved through the educational system and out into the world of work that it is not entirely surprising that its distinctive values and aspirations would affect in some measure these four organizations and the way they operate. The rapid growth of women and minorities in executive positions constitutes another set of influences. But organizations and their traditions are great disciplinarians over a lifetime, and it is uncertain how much the new generation of the organizations will eventually change. At best the changes are likely to be subtle. The influence of this new generation is introduced gradually, not all of a sudden as with the Lenin revolution.

SOME DEGREE OF CONVERGENCE

The developments and their consequences recounted above have disproportional impacts on the four types of organizations and their executives, but in general they also seem to be making the roles of executives somewhat more similar, or at least reducing their variance. For business enterprises, these developments are particularly relevant to "politically

[9] D.Q. Mills, *Business National Affairs,* "Daily Labor Report," September 10, 1986, p. A4.
[10] Ibid.

salient" industries in which executives have neither the unilateral authority nor unique competence to set policies on account of the diverse constituencies with which they must negotiate, often including governments.[11] Such industries are widespread, particularly in a more competitive international setting, and include enterprises in such sectors as automobiles, semiconductors, airframe, textiles, agribusiness, health care, and so on. In such settings executives are less and less able to follow closely the textbook of business strategic planning and decisionmaking. They are dependent upon their negotiations with U.S. governments over a wide range of questions including environmental standards and local taxes and subsidies, with foreign governments about overseas facilities, with labor organizations, and with financial institutions. In other ways, some business executives must deal with boycotts and other public demonstrations aroused by concern with investments in South Africa, by environmental advocacy, and the conditions of migrants on farms supplying raw material; for example, Campbell Soup Company. In these circumstances business executives appear less traditionally businesslike and reflect some affinity to the executives of government, academic institutions, and labor organizations. It is appropriate that the education of business executives includes more attention to these newer problems and involves more interaction with elements common to the training of executives in these other fields.[12]

One of the factors contributing to a degree of convergence among executives is the systematic development of

[11]Malcolm S. Salter, *Industrial Governance and Corporate Performance*, A Research Project of the Harvard Business School, May 1985, p. 20.
[12]John T. Dunlop, ed., *Business and Public Policy*, Cambridge, Harvard University Press, 1980, pp. 34–38 and 102–118.

multifaceted careers, particularly between the private sector (business, academia or labor organizations) and government. When the same individual has had executive responsibility in several fields there is a likelihood, although no certainty, that there may be less absolutism in the dealing among these organizations and more understanding of their internal processes and decisionmaking.[13] There are substantial impediments—financial, legal, educational and cultural—to dual careers in the public and private sectors. But there can be substantial benefits as Sol Linowitz urges: "I believe it would serve both the nation and the enterprise community if more people in the private sector spent some part of their careers in government service. A businessman who has worked for the government and brings his understanding of that world back to the private sector makes a real contribution to his company. And while serving the government he can make a special contribution to his country, provided that he has moved into a different national subculture with different purposes."[14]

There have long been some exchanges between academic careers and government; wartimes have expanded this exchange as it did with the business executive community. An early experience in the World War I period was that of Frank W. Taussig, Harvard economist, on the Tariff Commission and the Price-Fixing Committee of the War Industries Board. The New Deal and World War II initiated a broad flow. The first Ph.D. to serve in the Cabinet was

---

[13]Winthrop Knowlton and Richard Zeckhauser, eds., *American Society, Public and Private Responsibilities*, Cambridge, Mass., Ballinger Publishing Company, 1986.

[14]Sol Linowitz, *The Making of a Public Man*, Boston, Little Brown, 1985, p. 241.

Postmaster John A. Gronowski under President Lyndon Johnson (1963-65), and in my period (1975) there were five in the Cabinet.

Among labor leaders there have been far fewer appointments to executive posts in national government for a variety of reasons. A notable exception is the case of Thomas R. Donahue, now secretary-treasurer of the AFL-CIO, who served as an assistant secretary of the Department of Labor in the 1960s. This experience, in my view, served the government well and contributed significantly to the development of a ranking labor executive. A greater exchange of able talent from private sectors with government is vital to the development of effective public administration in a democratic society.

A comment needs to be made about executives of business trade associations, academic associations, and labor union federations as compared to executives in the constituent organization within each field. The ideal type of organization in each field does not characterize the confederation level. The executives of the Chamber of Commerce, the National Association of Manufacturers, the Association of State Legislators, the American Association of Universities, or the AFL-CIO have less freedom of decision than most of the constituent organizations on many issues that would affect the constituent members. Thus they tend to behave even more as mediators than the executives of affiliated organizations that are ordinarily free to leave the confederation at will. Moreover, many executives of constituent organizations may do poorly as leaders of confederations. For instance, John L. Lewis and Walter Reuther were great leaders of national unions but not so effective as executives of confederations. The functions and skills of the two levels of governance are quite different.

BIBLIOGRAPHY

Chester, I. Barnard, *The Functions of the Executive*, Cambridge, Harvard University Press, 1942.

Derek Bok, *Higher Learning*, Cambridge, Harvard University Press, 1986.

Derek C. Bok and John T. Dunlop, *Labor and the American Community*, New York, Simon and Schuster, 1970. See pp. 138-88 on the administration of unions.

Joseph L. Bower, *The Two Faces of Management, An American Approach to Leadership in Business and Politics*, Boston, Houghton Mifflin Company, 1983.

Alfred D. Chandler, Jr., *Strategy and Structure, Chapters in the History of the Industrial Enterprise*, Cambridge, Mass., M.I.T. Press, 1962; *The Visible Hand, The Managerial Revolution, Public Interest and the Private Role*, New York, Harper and Row, Publishers, 1984.

John T. Dunlop, ed., *Business and Public Policy*, Cambridge, Harvard University Press, 1980; *Dispute Resolution, Negotiation and Consensus Building*, Dover, Mass., Auburn House Publishing Company, 1984; "Public Management," September 25, 1979.

Davis Dyer, Malcolm S. Salter and Alan M. Webber, *Changing Alliances*, Boston, Harvard Business School Press, 1987.

Walter Galenson, *The United Brotherhood of Carpenters, The First Hundred Years*, Cambridge, Harvard University Press, 1983.

John W. Gardner, *Leadership Papers*: "The Nature of Leadership"; "The Tasks of Leadership"; "The Heart of the Matter, Leader-Constituent Interaction"; and "Leadership and Power," sponsored by Independent Sector, 1986.

Robert Aaron Gordon, *Business Leadership in the Large Corporation*, Washington, D.C., The Brookings Institution, 1945.

Hugh Heclo, *A Government of Strangers, Executive Politics in Washington*, Washington, D.C., The Brookings Institution, 1977.

Stuart Bruce Kaufman, Ed., *The Samuel Gompers Papers*, Vol. 1, *The Making of a Union Leader*, 1850-86, Urbana, University of Illinois Press, 1986.

Clark Kerr and Marian L. Gade, *The Many Lives of American Presidents, Time, Place and Character*, Washington, D.C., Association of Governing Boards of Universities and Colleges, 1986; Clark Kerr, *The Uses of the University*, Cambridge, Harvard University Press, 1963.

Winthrop Knowlton and Richard Zeckhauser, eds., *American Society, Public and Private Responsibilities*, Cambridge, Mass., Ballinger Publishing Company, 1986.

C. Wright Mills, *The New Men of Power, America's Labor Leaders*, New York, Harcourt Brace and Company, 1948.

Roger Porter, *Presidential Decision Making*, New York, Cambridge University Press, 1980.

Howard Rosen, *Servants of the People, The Uncertain Future of the Federal Civil Service*, Salt Lake City, Olympus Publishing Company, 1985.

Jerome M. Rosow, Ed., *Teamwork, Joint Labor-Management Programs in America*, New York, Pergamon Press, Work in America Institute, 1986.

Malcolm S. Salter, *Industrial Governance and Corporate Per-*

formance, A Research Project of the Harvard Business School, May 1985.

William H. Whyte, *The Organization Man*, 1956.

For-Profit Enterprise in Health Care, Committee on Implications of For-Profit Enterprise in Health Care, Institute of Medicine, Washington, D.C., National Academy Press, 1986.

CHAPTER EIGHT

Corporate Leadership and the Public Weal

MITCHELL SVIRIDOFF
AND
RENEE BERGER

While he was still at the helm of duPont, Irving Shapiro expounded the following position on the rising public posture of his fellow CEOs:

> The day is gone when the top of the organization chart permitted a private lifestyle. . . . A generation or two in the past, you could get by in business by following four rules: stick to business, stay out of trouble, join the right clubs, and don't talk to reporters.[1]

Lee Iacocca has since made the same point at greater length: Corporate leadership is no longer a matter of minding the store and avoiding the cameras. Creative leadership now has almost as much to do with the world outside the corporation as with the increasingly large and complex world within.

As the operating scale of major corporations increases, the prominence of the CEO has expanded exponentially, and has come more and more to resemble that of many mayors or governors. Their domains—measured both by the number of people they lead and by the resources at their command—dwarf those of prominent government leaders. The Fortune 500 account for $70 billion in profits and "govern" (the term is jarring but very much to the point) some 14 million employees.

Still, all of this only suggests that the CEO is nowadays a public figure of some note. It doesn't necessarily follow that corporate executives should *court* such public recognition, or that they should move any further into the arena of public affairs than the force of their status and their

[1]"Business and the Public Policy Process," *Business and Public Policy*, John T. Dunlop, ed., Cambridge, Harvard University Press, 1980, p. 29.

company's direct business interests propel them. More to the point, the involvement of businesses and their managers in areas of traditional government responsibility involving day care, education, housing, and other public services does not follow solely from the fact that executive leadership now brings with it a degree of public visibility and influence.

Yet more and more business leaders appear to have reached the conclusion that their companies' interests—or at least their own—lie to some degree in the arena of public affairs. They have taken this position in opposition to a certain amount of cautious advice from a few management critics. Milton Friedman, for one, felt strongly about this issue when he wrote:

> Few trends could so thoroughly undermine the very foundations of our free society as the acceptance by corporate officials of a social responsibility other than to make as much money for their stockholders as possible.[2]

However much one might have hoped for a more delicate turn of phrase, Friedman's objection does raise a challenge to the national trend—promoted by both government and corporate leaders—toward more business involvement in public affairs. What business do businesspeople have in matters that were once the domain of Church and State? How does a corporate role in charitable or governmental activities (other than as a vendor, contractor, ratepayer, or lobbyist) benefit the stockholders, employees and customers to whom every business is in the first instance beholden? And what good is such involvement for the public?

[2]Milton Friedman, *Capitalism and Freedom,* Chicago, University of Chicago Press, 1962, p. 133.

Before we can answer these questions with any confidence, we might do well to consider how the roles of business and government came to overlap, and what (if anything) should be done about it.

THREE CENTURIES OF PUBLIC INVOLVEMENT

America 300 years ago was a simple society. Business, government, and religion enjoyed roles and obligations that were relatively stable, at least in theory and often in practice. This was the period when de Tocqueville observed Americans' willingness to extend time and money to help neighbors and the less fortunate.

All three of these fundamental institutions were rooted in communities whose average population would not have filled New York's Metropolitan Opera House, much less the typical American city of the 1980s. The modern corporation did not exist. A businessperson's civic responsibility was the same as anyone else's: to participate in public activities as an individual and to extend a little charity either from pocket or cash till, if the need presented itself.

Otherwise, the role of business was to make profits, thereby meeting its primary social obligation: to ensure a booming local economy. Government, put simply, existed to provide a setting in which private initiative could prosper. This tranquil vision lasted nearly 100 years.

By the end of the Civil War and lasting until the late 1960s, America saw the creation of wealth and power, both in individuals and organizations, that came more and more to dominate or at least influence the welfare of an increasingly metropolitan and technological society. Governments, corporations, and private foundations expanded their activities in a climate that seemed to speed both progress and hubris. Business's primary responsibility was still to generate profits, but the scale of corporations, the size of the corporate workforce, and the dangerous side effects of new manufacturing technologies soon came to raise public expectations and demands that business executives had never before faced. These forces provided the spark for unionization. They also encouraged the rise of the American philanthropist.

With sudden and vast wealth of proportions known before only to nobility, people like Andrew Carnegie, John D. Rockefeller, and Andrew Mellon began to invent a uniquely American noblesse *oblige*. Carnegie's essay, "The Gospel of Wealth," asserted that the rich were obligated to become philanthropists. By taking on such responsibility, the affluent would produce "an ideal state in which the surplus wealth of the few would become, in the best sense, the property of the many." The newly wealthy created a vehicle for sharing their economic rewards: the foundation.

Late in this second American century, philanthropists and their businesses came more and more to take a role in meeting charitable needs once confined to families and religious bodies. By the mid-1930s, corporate contributions to social and charitable activities had reached almost .4 percent of net profit. Though this amounted only to some $30 million dollars a year, it was a beginning. Donations went mainly for hospitals, community chests, and human service agencies like the YMCA. Corporate giving to education, which would increase rapidly after 1950, was still relatively modest.

But government also grew in this period, both in its overall scope and in its involvement in social and charitable issues. This growth began with local governments, but quickly spread to the federal level beginning with the New Deal.

The 1960s represented a watershed both for government as well as for business. Behind the more sensational War on Poverty was also a trend that many considered a war on profit: a growing policy of suspicion toward corporations, which eventually led to a bull market for government regulators and watchdogs in areas like environmental quality, consumer protection, fairness in lending and insurance, in hiring the disadvantaged, and in contracting with minority suppliers and vendors. Corporations were routinely on the defensive.

Finally, in the 1970s, the Carter Administration attempted to quiet what had become a strained relationship between business and government, by introducing the notion of "public-private partnership." The cornerstone of this approach was in urban policy (where so much of the earlier adversity had been concentrated). Before long it had spread to employment policy. By the coming of the Reagan Administration, it had become possible for the federal government itself (and a distinctly pro-business government) to urge on the nation's manufacturers, merchants, and service companies a greater role in meeting social needs.

Since 1980, we have seen a dramatic rise in both monetary and nonmonetary contributions by corporations. Cash contributions, which as already noted averaged just $30 million yearly in the 1930s, reached $2.3 billion in 1980 and grew to $4.3 billion by 1985—an increase of 87 percent in the 5-year period. The exhortations of the federal government may have hastened this increase. More likely, increased profits, government retrenchment, and the resulting growth in the needs of charitable groups led to most of the upsurge in corporate public involvement.

But the point of this highly truncated history becomes clear when we ask how a tradition of corporate noblesse oblige, by now more than a century old, matches the demands of the modern corporation, and the needs of a society that, even after the Reagan revolution, finds government spending half a trillion dollars on social problems and programs. In other words, what conceivable contribution can corporate charity—monetary or otherwise—make in the midst of a social need and a public commitment of these proportions? What does it benefit either corporations or government that some businesses make socially motivated sacrifices which, at their highest level in history, still amount to only a tiny percent of the amount that government spends on these purposes?

WHO GIVES HOW MUCH TO WHAT?

The multibillion dollar contributions of corporations in 1985 were awarded mainly to education, health, youth, and other human-service organizations. Since 1975, education and human services have received more than 70 percent of all corporate contributions.

But outright cash contribution is only one approach to resource distribution. The total dollar value of corporate expenditures on charitable activities, including professional time and other in-kind contributions (as opposed to outright grants), is not monitored. The Conference Board's estimates, however, suggest that the $4.3 billion figure would increase dramatically, perhaps double, if these non-cash gifts were included.

In its "Annual Survey of Corporate Contributions" for 1986, the Conference Board also suggests that business contributions may be focused more and more on the physical and economic condition of their communities: environmental, housing, and economic development programs particularly. Economic development, a broad category that includes national as well as neighborhood organizations concerned with employment, housing and other forms of long-term development, now receives around 5 percent of overall corporate giving.

The Conference Board's picture, interesting as it is, nevertheless only describes the contributions of large companies, whose grants may individually be the most dramatic but do not account for the whole of corporate philanthropy. As we noted before, cash figures do not include the value of the time of loaned executives, donated professional space, equipment, and administrative services, which made up a large part of corporate assistance to nonprofit organizations, and of the corporate share in public-private collaborative endeavors. Further, so-called "socially-responsible investments," which the Center for Corporate Public Involvement estimated to be more than $1.3 billion in 1985 in the insurance industry alone, are also not counted as part of corporate contributions. These special investments, which over the past 15 years have come to carve out their own niche in the financial-services industry, represent varying degrees of business commitment to goals other than those of profit and competition. The picture, in short, is a big one—bigger than even the largest published numbers suggest.

HOW MUCH IS ENOUGH?

Since 1936, the Internal Revenue Code has allowed corporations to deduct contributions to charitable organizations up to a maximum of 5 percent of the corporation's taxable income, with a 5-year carry-forward. Provisions in the

Economic Recovery Act of 1981 raised the limit to 10 percent. Given that taxable income is a closely guarded figure among most companies, the standard practice has been to express corporate contributions in terms of pre-tax net income.

Until recently—for more than 20 years, in fact—contributions as a percentage of pretax net income had hovered around 1 percent. The very consistency of this figure over time seems to suggest that it has been used, formally or informally, as a guide in setting contributions budgets. In 1973, the Commission on Private Philanthropy and Public Needs (known as the Filer Commission, after its chairman, John Filer, who was then also the chairman of Aetna Life & Casualty) recommended that "corporations set as a minimum goal, to be reached no later than 1980, the giving to charitable organizations 2 percent of pretax net income." Again, in 1982, the President's Task Force on Private Sector Initiatives issued a recommendation urging businesses to double their level of cash giving within four years, a goal that paralleled the two percent of the Filer Commission.

These recommendations may have had their effect. Contributions have lately climbed to 1.89 percent from a 1980 level of 1.01 percent. In this climate, Independent Sector, an association of organizations dedicated to stimulating giving and volunteering generally, has started to instigate measurable growth coalitions among local nonprofit organizations, foundations, and corporations in 15 cities or more. Independent Sector's national goal for these coalitions will be to double the 1985 level of all giving by 1991, and to increase hours of volunteering by 50 percent. If they succeed, for corporate giving in particular, it would bring the total, at present profit levels, to $8.6 billion.

A GLANCE AT THE FUTURE

For some, the crusade will not be over until levels of 5 percent or more come into view; for others (presumably those who share Milton Friedman's view), the first dollar of corporate charity paves the way to madness and the whole exercise is simply an extravaganza.

In the foreseeable future the corporate-contribution bears may be closer to the mark. There are at least three good reasons that even relatively progressive corporations may find themselves less committed to expanding their involvement than they have been in the past. All the rationales for corporate activism—many of them good ones—will nonetheless have to cope sooner or later with powerful market forces that threaten at least to stem the expansion, and possibly to reverse it:

1. The Slow Growth and Instability of the Economy

Except in the recent salad days of corporate activism, most increases in social involvement by business have closely paralleled economic growth. As profits have risen and businesses have expanded, so have contributions and social involvement. The current picture does not give much hope for the steady growth and long-term optimism that would be expected to underlie a lasting expansion in corporate giving. The tendency toward globalization of the economy and the shifting stakes caused by mounting mergers, acquisitions and restructurings have made the business environment so unstable that despite signs of greater strength, the toehold of corporate social activity may well prove to be fragile.

2. A New Tax Environment

Among the many questions presented by the tax code revisions of 1986 will be the range of effects that a corporate contribution will have on a company's tax bill in 1987 and beyond. It is certainly possible to overstate the matter: Corporate contributions have rarely, if ever, been primarily motivated by considerations of tax benefit. Still, a change in the system of tax benefits—particularly an adverse change, or even a neutral but confusing one—could well discourage new activity and provide top management with the incentive to rethink existing policies.

3. The Shrinking Time Horizon

This is the most speculative consideration, but possibly the most relevant. It has generally been believed—especially given the recent tendency to compare government with corporate management—that the strength of top business management is its ability to take the long view. Government, by contrast, looks necessarily to the next headline, the next fiscal year, the next election. But lately the horizon has begun to move in on corporate executives. Constant pressure from corporate raiders, Wall Street analysts, and the press (to say nothing of increasingly vocal shareholders) all seem to be conspiring to make the executive suite function more and more like City Hall. That is the other side of the public profile Irving Shapiro described in our opening quotation: The day in which a few canny executives could make near-term sacrifices for a long-range return, and expect to enjoy some insulation and independence in the process, may well be over. Even though it is extremely rare for stockholders (or anyone else) to complain about the corporate contribution program, the shrinking time horizon of the contemporary CEO makes it more difficult to justify an aggressive public involvement strategy.

The public-involvement bulls, on the other hand, believe that these deterrents are temporary, that the current problems are transitory, and that when certain wrenching adjustments in the economy are completed, business will return to a healthier condition—one more conducive to long-term planning and socially-responsible behavior. They also believe that the corporation's sense of responsibility to the social compact, which undergirds American capitalism, and the human impulse to give, both exist independent of the bottom line. Time will tell whether these motivational factors are that powerful.

These issues bring us full circle to the question that suggested itself at the beginning of this discussion: What forces could persuade a modern CEO, especially one facing the constraints that have emerged over the past few years, to involve his or her company in social problems outside the company's regular lines of business? And if such forces exist, as they seem to, what real benefit can corporations that respond anticipate?

PUBLIC AND PRIVATE:
A BORDER DISPUTE WITHOUT A BORDER

The Reagan Administration's blunt talk about the role of the free market, and its use of the corporate boardroom as the ideal model of government management, whatever their merits, have heightened an already ideological debate about the roles of the public and private sectors. Just as the government needs to be more businesslike, the argument emphasizes, so must business be more actively a part of public affairs.

In 1981, President Reagan introduced a "private sector initiatives" policy to promote corporate community involvement and volunteering. It was on the heels of the Omnibus Budget Reconciliation Act, which cut federal domestic programs. Whether the two events were connected in the Administration's strategy, their timing made it difficult to see them as anything other than linked. The government intended to spend less on social problems, and concomitantly expected the business sector to spend more.

The arithmetic of this trade-off made it instantly clear that the shift would be philosophical at most: $38 billion in government cuts was not about to be replaced by corporate philanthropy, which never amounted to more than a tenth of the sum being withdrawn, or by volunteering. The point was rather that the government wished to transfer a large category of social activity to private hands, whether through charity, churches, or community organizations. And those private agencies would have to find more private funds than they ever did before. Executives of numerous nonprofit social service agencies quickly pointed out their capacity to meet such broadened social needs would be so limited that their future was in jeopardy.

In the midst of this confusion, William S. Woodside, chairman of the American Can Corporation, summed up the problem for corporate executives: "The private sector can help, but the basic leadership, commitment, and funding must come from the government. It is unconscionable to expect business to provide funds of the magnitude supplied in the past by government in areas of major social concern to the United States."[3]

However one may judge the Reagan Administration's sense of proportion, it was certainly appropriate for it to encourage the collaboration of business and government on problems that are, in themselves, neither solely public nor private. For example, if the educational system cannot deliver literate workers, or if working parents are kept out of the labor force for lack of child care, it is a moot question whether the problem is of more concern to the private or the public sector.

Furthermore, the two sectors bring substantially different kinds (not just amounts) of resources to the solution of such problems. Government can fund broad, general, immediate activities based on calculations of public acceptance. But only at some remove from the glare of politics (and with some access to technical expertise as well as money) can an organization provide the innovation, development, experimentation, evaluation, and collaboration that underlie the creation of better public policies. That happens primarily in the private sector. Particularly when such policy affects the future performance of the labor market, national productivity, and civic stability, the more experimental efforts in informing public policy (the R and D, so to speak) work best outside of government.

We should not treat this point lightly. On it rests most of the answer to the question we have been raising. If it is true that some so-called "public" policies affect business as much as (or more than) other parts of society; and if it is also true that businesses and foundations can bring unique resources to improving such policies, then the stake of the

[3]*New York Times*, Monday, April 28, 1986, p. D3.

private sector in the public arena becomes clearer and more compelling.

CORPORATE PUBLIC INVOLVEMENT: A COST OF DOING BUSINESS

Economic purists, as we have seen, will argue that stockholders' interests are served by investment policies that maximize the market value of their stock, presumably in the near term. When they do so, they seem to be ruling out not only a good portion of corporate public involvement, but a great many other promotion and development strategies that promise an intangible or long-term benefit to the company.

Without opening a discussion into the ways of measuring the value of long-term intangibles, these purists appear to be talking about much simpler worlds of ownership and governance, which in reality began to emerge sometime in the early part of this century. The modern stockholder, for example, holds interests in several companies and industries, or may participate in a diversified mutual fund. To these stockholders, activities that promote the smooth functioning of the economy and the stability of society are very much to the point. In what sense does the simple cash-investment/cash-return analysis serve all the interests of such an investor? The economic well being of corporations is clearly related to the stability of our social and political arrangements. By applying corporate skills and resources to the business of ensuring that stability—particularly when few other skills and resources are available or effective—the corporate manager responds directly to stockholders' needs.

Some social-responsibility evangelists of the old school,

as well meaning as they are, miss the point just as much as the economic purists. The era of American corporate *noblesse oblige* is in its twilight. The modern corporation, with a few interesting exceptions, is no longer sufficiently identified with the values of a particular person or family to respond actively to this tradition. The charitable impulse—the desire to do good for the less fortunate—is a fundamental, personal urge; it comes from the identification of one human being with the hardships of another. The modern corporation is nowadays rarely an emanation of any single human being. And no matter how charitable are the impulses of the people who run the company, the company itself offers no particular advantages as a vehicle to their charitable desires. Personal philanthropy by the wealthy no longer blends with their businesses.

So if the stake of business in social improvement and stability is more than just charitable, it must lie in the interests of good business, simply and directly. And so it does. Like the public official, the corporate executive must juggle the needs of different constituencies. Increasingly, as regulation imposes social considerations on ordinary day-to-day business (consider the financial or chemical industries for example), and as public pressure demands greater participation by business in public affairs, one of the principal constituencies of the modern corporate executive is the community at large. But that constituency does not merely represent a potential danger in the form of new regulation or new polemics in the press, it also represents the seed bed of future labor, future customers, and future lines of business.

The community thereby takes its place alongside stockholders and employees as part of the world to which the corporation, and the CEO, is accountable. Enlightened companies therefore contribute in their own best interests to the well being of this constituency. Having said that, we must be quick to put some limits on the point, which can all too easily be overstated in the interests of an ideological transfer of government responsibility to private hands. The interests of business—and of business's stakeholders, including the community at large—are not served by an ill defined, boundless corporate generosity extending itself into every area of community need. The corporate sector has neither the resources nor the skill to assume any large portion of the nearly half-trillion dollars in the federal government's social programs. What then is the corporation's social or public role?

Along with other institutions with a heavy stake in public stability and progress—unions, private foundations, and universities, for example—its role is to advance the human condition through support of innovation, experimentation, research, analysis, interpretation, the strengthening of collaborative efforts, and the development of community leadership. It is also to help keep alive the dynamic pluralism and diversity in human service and cultural institutions that distinguish and enrich American life. It is to behave in ways that reinforce the social contract between centers of wealth and power and the community. It is only in such an environment that free enterprise can continue to flourish, and to keep at arm's length the inroads of governmental centralization that even the most welfare-minded European societies have recently begun to question.

Hence, the role that corporations have traditionally taken in influencing public policy around their own lines of business is also the role they must take—and increasingly do take—in the formulation and support of public policy as it affects the public weal. To do so has become an inescapable part of the cost of their doing business and not simply an act of old-fashioned charity.

As in most things, some players are more successful than others. The great majority of corporations do not yet have a vision of their public role that approaches what we have just described. The leaders in corporate public involvement—people of the stature of Irving Shapiro, John Filer or William Woodside—are still a minority of corporate CEOs, even as the amount of corporate money flowing into public efforts grows dramatically.

Yet corporate involvement in social, philanthropic, or other kinds of public activity has already eclipsed that of private foundations. If one includes a reasonable estimate of in-kind contributions and socially motivated investments, the amount of corporate activity already outstrips foundations by perhaps two or three to one. If current trends continue, it will not be long before cash contributions alone—traditional corporate philanthropy—exceed the level of all the grant budgets of independent foundations combined. That means that the bulk of the philanthropic money in circulation is, or will soon be, corporate money. How it is used by the CEOs who control it will determine whether corporations assume a major role in the shaping of future public policy and social stability.

So far, many are using it for a rather limited form of corporate publicity (which may well prove to be one of the least effective approaches to advertising, relative to the cost). Others contribute and even participate in various public efforts as a way of bowing to peer pressure—putting out a little money because not to do so would be conspicuous. Some others are still acting from an honest (if slightly antiquarian) sense of *noblesse oblige*, dribbling out small amounts across a wide field of social and charitable programs. However benevolent these actions may be in spirit, they are all the wrong reasons for public involvement by corporations. And while they do no harm, they frequently do no particular good either. They represent a small view of a large and growing role for corporations and their executives. Like all small means, they are destined to produce small ends, or no ends at all.

For the most part, executives whose view of their public role is narrow tend to relegate that role to management at low levels, to people of limited imagination and skill. Their inclination to think of public involvement as an expenditure without a return is then reinforced by the insignificant results that usually come from management without a vision or focus.

Chief executive officers, however, who take their public role seriously and tackle it creatively, recognize that their companies' public involvement budgets are major devices for influencing the well being of the wider community from which their next generation of stockholders, employees and regulators will come. They will therefore place this responsibility in senior and responsible hands and accord it an importance equal to that of their other two major stakeholders: employees and investors. A corporate executive's ability to use his or her time, energy, and skill in a balanced and mutually reinforcing way to respond to the interests of all three stakeholders will be one of the acid tests of corporate leadership.

CHAPTER NINE

Tomorrow's Executives:
Findings and
Directions for Research

ELI GINZBERG

As noted in the Preface, the stimulus for this volume derived from the belief shared by members of the Advisory Council of the Career Center at the Graduate School of Business at Columbia University that it would be useful to elicit contributions from leading academicians and practitioners of human resources policies in contemporary organizations to determine whether their views are congruent and could be regarded as an overview of current theory and practice. A second desideratum is to determine whether their contributions contain a number of important issues that might serve as suggestions and directions for young researchers in the field.

In this concluding chapter I shall address both challenges. In the identification and interpretations of their propositions about executives in the new world of work and in pointing the directions for research, the participating writers have no responsibility; the editor assumes sole responsibility for the propositions that he has drawn from their work and the use he has made of them in constructing a research agenda.

THE MAJOR PROPOSITIONS

1. The Human Resources Revolution: Key to Business Survival

Several themes recur throughout the preceding chapters: The economic environment has become more threatening even to the well run corporation; international competition is likely to intensify; the surest and shortest road to bankruptcy for a corporation is to resist all change; organizations must modify their structures and decision-making processes so they can respond more effectively to the new environment; the greatest challenge resides in the management of people. People are the key asset in every organization; and if they are not encouraged to use their talents and skills, the organization will not achieve its goals and will perish.

George Vojta in Chapter 2 remarks that most senior managers must learn how to release the latent capabilities of their workforces and to insure that their efforts are focused on priority goals. To achieve this release and focus requires a sophisticated human resources policy. Such a policy can be created only by mature executives who understand business strategy and how the work scene can be restructured. Vojta is the first of many contributors to observe that most personnel departments are not equipped to lead the much delayed revolution in human resources.

2. The Neglect of Human Resources in Strategic Planning

Economics students are taught that the corporate form of enterprise was initiated in the 19th century in response to the need for organizations to endure beyond the lifetime of the founder, and to draw on talent and skills outside the founder's immediate family. In contemporary multibillion dollar corporations, founders and their heirs often own less than 1 percent of the stock; rarely do they own as much as 5 percent. The successful operation of these macro business institutions is based on the selection, training, and promotion of middle and senior managers and on the senior executives whose decision-making skills determine the ability of the corporation to prosper in response to new challenges and opportunities.

It is anomalous that the executives who have the primary responsibility for safeguarding and enhancing these valuable assets have not been more successful in their attempts to include their corporation's human resources in their strategic planning. Boris Yavitz in Chapter 3 offers as his first of two principal explanations for this shortcoming the long-term inclination of prototypical manufacturers to view human resources as a homogenized commodity in ample supply in the labor market, to be hired when needed and furloughed or discharged when the demand for the firm's product declines. The view of labor as a variable cost has persisted in part because most employees in manufacturing have been and still are engaged in relatively simple physical manipulations. In recent years, however, a much higher proportion of the workforce consists of "knowledge workers"—managerial, professional, and technical workers—whose understanding of the company—its products, markets, policies, and procedures—is not readily replaced.

Yavitz's second explanation for the failure of senior corporate executives to deal with human resources as a strategic element derives from the contemporary accounting profession that, while it has developed sophisticated techniques for tracing and evaluating flows of financial resources, has been slow to impute values to such assets as the corporation's human resources. Yavitz is cautiously optimistic that at both the corporate and the subsidiary levels, senior executives, under the stimuli of enhanced competitiveness, worldwide sourcing, and improved information systems, will recognize the need to modify their strategic planning methodologies to include human resources. There would be little profit to my offering a partial disclaimer to his measured optimism. But I will call attention to the hurdles that first must be lowered.

The first exists in the time horizons that continue to

dominate most U.S. corporations. Chief executive officers are concerned mainly with their quarterly reports of sales and profits, rather than the longer term scope and faraway rewards of human resources planning.

There is a second potent reason that improved understanding and better methodologies may not assure that human resources planning is given its appropriate place in strategic planning. The important difference between financial and human capital is that the former can be separated from its owner, but human talents and skills are embedded in the individual. Rather, human emotions are always engaged in power struggles; senior executives may be unwilling to increase the number of people involved in the selection and promotion of key associates. Executives who seek to strengthen their own positions, as most executives do, may not support the establishment of a strong human resources function if they believe that might reduce their authority to select their associates and key subordinates.

3. The Unfilled Promise of the Human Resources Function

In Chapter 4 Stephen Drotter inquires whether, if senior executives were to give the human resources function its head, it would deliver. His careful answer is based on his experience of many decades with three major corporations and his consulting experiences with many more.

He is not certain that human resources staffs have the potential to respond. He is certain, however, that to respond meaningfully the function must be transformed radically.

The following is an abbreviated list of some of the major shortcomings of the human resources function:

It is inadequately staffed for both university recruitment and for overseeing corporate assignments.

Its basic philosophy is reactive instead of proactive.

The relationship between the head of the function and the CEO is distorted because the former often acts as "valet" to "master".

The solution to tactical problems commands most of the function's time and resources.

The development and training of people are undervalued.

Many human resources groups serve as complaint departments and attempt to act as a buffer for workers' and middle managers' discontent.

Drotter notes the although the human resources function is inadequate today, it will be even more inadequate tomorrow as business confronts an increasingly complex competitive environment.

What can be done? Drotter makes a strong case for the human resources group's shifting attention from the supply to the demand side, defined as follows: how many workers are needed; how work should be organized; what skills are required; how the organization should be structured. In most businesses, the human resources staff is not even asked for its opinions on these matters.

Drotter concludes his critical analysis by explaining the need for corporations to shift from a system of "control" of people to one of employee self-management; from assuming that the individual employee will put forth his or her best performance to establish the environment that will elicit such behavior. If many believe as I did before reading Drotter's chapter that his term "dinosaur" was unduly pejorative, I suspect they may now agree that the present

circumstances are bleak and the human resources departments may well become extinct.

4. Corporations Must Change

Kirby Warren's discussion of corporate restructuring in
Chapter 5 can be considered as a special case of Vojta's
analysis emphasizing the impact of an organization's realities on its human resources. Warren puts and answers the
difficult question about how misalignments between organizational structures and patterns of human resources utilization can be realigned after changes in the market have
undermined the preexisting relationships. Warren limits his
exploration to large U.S. corporations, but his line of inquiry
is applicable to the large corporation and small, as well as to
organizations not engaged in profit-making pursuits.

Warren's point of departure is the historical circumstances that led to the overstaffing of the middle management ranks of U.S. corporations during the period of 1945 to
1970, a time when most operated at home and abroad with
little competition since the other major participants in
World War II were rebuilding their economies while newly
independent nations were launching their own economic
development programs.

The underlying theme in Warren's analysis is that most
large corporations understood too late that they face a new
and more intense competitive environment and that they
must divest themselves of their surplus managerial personnel through such methods as early retirement, golden handshakes, golden windows, and across-the-board and selective reductions in force. The thrust of his argument is not
that in difficult times excess personnel must be eliminated,
but that in periods of rapid change only the corporation that

attempts to restructure itself is likely to survive and prosper. Warren points the path for such a restructuring effort: The senior executives need to decide on the business and the markets in which they will be involved five years out. They must explore alternative configurations that will enable them to meet this challenge. Restructuring cannot be effected quickly. It requires clarifying future goals, the elements of the new structure, and the implementation steps that will move the company from its future configuration to its present reality.

5. Young Managers are Different

Successive generations of any population group tend to change in response to altered circumstances of their families, their developmental experiences, and their encounters in the adult society they eventually join. The values of both the individual and the society are always subject to change; in the post-World War II years, values were transformed rapidly in response to such radically new conditions as the threat of nuclear extinction, the sexual revolution, substantial increases in formal educational preparation, and the women's movement.

The study of values is not easy, and changes in values that correlate with changes in managers' and executives' goals and behavior are even more complex. Fortunately however, AT&T in the heyday of its security and stability (mid 1950s) initiated a unique longitudinal study of its newly hired managers and replicated the effort in the late 1970s.

The author of Chapter 6, Dr. Douglas Bray, served as the long-term director of Human Resources Research for AT&T; and is therefore uniquely qualified to report on the rich results from these carefully designed and executed investigations, which are without parallel in this country or abroad. As Bray notes, there are reasons to believe that his findings apply to many large U.S. corporations; they are not idiosyncratic to the communications utility now dismembered.

In the first (1950s) study, trainees were seen as enthusiastic and ambitious; they had high expectations about moving up the managerial and executive ladder. Some fulfilled their expectations; most did not. The new group (late 1970s) had less ambition and were less motivated to lead. They are not as optimistic about their roles as managers or about the company. Only one in five was confident that conflicts between job and family could be avoided. This recent group scored higher on general mental ability but lower on interpersonal skills.

Bray points out that the latter survey subjects were just as interested in good pay, challenging work, and quality performance as their predecessors. He surmises, however, that in the years ahead they will demonstrate a lower drive to advance.

In the face of weakened corporate commitments to middle and higher managers, Bray raises the critical question about whether the corporation of tomorrow will be able to elicit the quantity and quality of effort that it will require to compete successfully in the unstable environment that now characterizes all business enterprises. It is a good question, to which few would give a ringing affirmative reply.

6. Different Executives for Different Organizations

It is said that citizens of a democracy get the type of leadership they deserve. Consider the following: It is difficult for

an "outsider" to be nominated for the U.S. presidency—
Wendell Wilkie was the last such outsider (1940) in that he
had held no prior elected or appointed public office. The
presidency makes demands on the incumbent unlike any
other position in American life. But this book is not focused
on such a unique function as the nation's chief executive: It
addresses issues involved in the selection and performance
of senior managers in important organizations in different
sectors, including corporate, government, trade union, and
academic.

John T. Dunlop analyzed in Chapter 7 how different
organizational structures and missions influence and determine the types of executives that rise to the top. He traced
some of the ways in which these organizational imperatives
determine the goals that different executives pursue and
their approaches to realizing them.

Dunlop singles out six key dimensions of organizational
activities that set the bonds within which executives
operate:

The measures used to assess their performance—which
range from profits to votes;

The tensions between efficiency and equity, with the
business executive often forced to focus more on the
former;

The reliance on command versus persuasion, with the
former playing a larger role in business than in other
organizations;

The extent to which senior executives are constrained by
tradition, with corporate and trade union executives
enjoying the greater degrees of freedom; and

The role of time in their management decisions, in which
political leaders face the shortest horizon, academic and
trade union leaders the longest.

One major distillation from Dunlop's comparative analysis is that errors result from any analysis that fails to include the ways in which organizational (and environmental) conditions shape and influence the selection and the work of senior executives. Put differently, Dunlop's analysis is a warning against the common error of formulating an "ideal" type of executive and assuming that this concept can be employed fruitfully in assessing executive performance across different organizations.

In the concluding section of his chapter, Dunlop addresses the degree of convergence among executives of different organizational entities. He points particularly to two developments: the extent to which many corporations are intertwined with various government entities—consider multinationals, aerospace companies, the disinvestment issue in South Africa—and the considerable career mobility of many executives among business, government, and the universities. It is my impression that academics and lawyers have been more successful in making career shifts into government and out again than have corporate officials who moved into senior government positions or senior bureaucrats or high-ranking military officers who moved into the corporate or academic worlds.

7. The Balance Between Flexibility and Caution

In Chapter 8 Mitchell Sviridoff and Renee Berger focused on the tantalizing theme of how corporate executives respond with dollars and voluntary labor to social needs in their communities. The authors trace the role of philanthropy in American life, how the large corporation first entered the philanthropic arena and the significant role it has come to play, although that role remains much smaller than the dollars from government. The most striking statistic they present is the rise in annual corporate philanthropic dollars, from $2.3 billion in 1980 to $4.3 billion in 1985, dollars directed primarily to human services and education.

In looking ahead, the authors are not sure that the recent rise in corporate philanthropic contributions, amounting to an approximate doubling of donations, is likely to continue at such a steep rate; but they do not rule out such a prospect. They are clear however that the corporate sector cannot make up the sizable cutbacks ($38 billion) made by the early Reagan administration in human services programs.

They conclude their analysis by citing new developments in corporate philanthropy. In their view the community takes its place alongside employees and stockholders as stakeholders to which "the corporation, and the CEO, are accountable." But they emphasize that the corporate sector has neither the resources nor the skill "to assume any large portion of the nearly half- trillion dollars in government social programs."

The authors of this chapter cite the differences among top executives: Some have recognized the opportunities that exist for mutual advantage when a corporation responds to one or another community need within its orbit of interest and capability. But they note that most executives have been slow to appreciate such challenges and even slower to respond to them.

To recapitulate, the following major themes have been extracted from the preceding chapters:

The human resources revolution: key to business survival

The neglect of human resources in strategic planning

The unfulfilled promise of the human resources function

Corporations must change
Young managers are different
Different executives for different organizations
Executives respond to their environment

Each of these themes points to the significant changes that are underway, internally and externally, exerting pressures on executives to realign their organizations so they can respond more effectively to the challenges and opportunities they face. There are two overriding themes that transcend the individual chapters and in one or another formulations are found in all of them: With markets and the external world undergoing rapid change, no organization can survive and prosper unless its structure and methods of operation are aligned with emerging trends. In facing this challenge, executives must reckon with the fact that their prospects of success depend largely on the extent to which the changes they introduce will be responsive to the expressed needs of a more capable workforce—junior, middle, and senior managers who want more responsibility to use their talents and skills and be rewarded accordingly.

DIRECTIONS FOR RESEARCH

In the Preface I noted that one of the spurs to undertaking this collaborative effort was the need to provide young researchers in the human resources field with a selective appreciation of the thematic changes that are underway and to chart some directions for research. Accordingly, in this section I offer some pointers to open issues embedded in the thematic propositions that have just be reviewed. Addressing these can add significantly to the existing pool of knowledge about human resources.

Can we identify either, in the United States or abroad, one or more corporations that have succeeded in making room in their strategic planning processes for human resources? Can their methodologies be described? Can their presumed gains be assessed?

There are significant differences in the approaches pursued by corporations, civilian government, the military, trade unions, universities, organized religious groups, foundations, and other organizations in their formal and informal methods of executive development. Query: What gains in deepened understanding and refined methodologies could result from a systematic comparative study of these different approaches to executive development?

Could we gain a fuller appreciation of the changing demands on senior executives by analyzing their appointment schedules of two decades ago (or through other devices) compared to the current distribution of their time and effort?

There are many impressions but few hard facts about the relative degrees of success of senior executives who move from one organization to another or within sectors. It should be easy to conduct a representative sample of such "mobile" executives over the past two to three decades that would provide the basis for moving from rough impressions to reliable conclusions.

The recent spate of acquisitions, mergers, and leveraged buyouts has been underway for a sufficient number of years that the consequent success/failure of many of these undertakings are now part of the public record. Query: What would the analysis of a structured sample of such investments reveal about the role of "human resources" in contributing to their success or failure?

During this decade many leading U.S. corporations have downsized their managerial ranks. What can an analysis of a structured sample tell us about the relative strengths and weaknesses of different methodologies geared to achieve short-term goals and long-term profits?

How can we explain the differences in corporate behavior in responding to community needs whereby some companies make insignificant contributions and others donate more than 2 percent of their before-tax income to such efforts? How do the more responsive corporations explain and justify their policies to their stockholders?

What lessons can be extracted from investment banking (and similar arenas where rewards are geared to contributions) that might have applicability to other businesses so that middle-level managers can be encouraged to perform at their highest potential and be rewarded accordingly?

Can we identify a number of different approaches with which corporations have experimented to offer alternative work contracts to junior and middle managers who prefer to commit less than full time to their employers? What preliminary assessments can be made concerning the advantage of such new arrangements for employer and employee alike?

What would a critical rereading and reanalysis of the genre of "pursuit of excellence" books reveal about the strengths and weaknesses of corporate performance in the light of recent developments?

During the last two decades there has been a spotty but considerable effort to increase the flow of women and minorities into middle and higher management in both the private and public sectors. In addition to analyzing critically the available macro data, it would be desirable to elicit the cooperation of a group of successful organizations to assess the methodologies they have used and to ascertain the limits of such approaches.

Sophisticated human resources specialists contend that their staffs should include a predominance of individuals with line experience. If this assumption is accepted, what would be the outlines of a professional recruiting-assignment-training-promotion program for assuring the requisite number of mature, senior human resources staffers?

The foregoing suggestions for future research have identified avenues of inquiry that are likely to result in opening up still more important new questions to be explored.

If, as the contributors to this book believe, human resources and particularly executives are the critical factor in organizational effectiveness; if our knowledge about them is deficient in relation to their role in organizational management, growth, and survival; if the challenges they face are increasing in number and complexity, then more and better research is a desideratum. Research will not provide all the knowledge we need to assure a higher level of organizational performance, but it should contribute to that end.

INDEX

Index

English language skills, 15
Environment, 22–23
  changes in, 5, 6–7, 120
Environmental scan, 50–51
Equality of opportunity, 5
Executive(s)
  academic, 118, 123, 125–128, 130–132, 134, 137–139
  changing characteristics of, 129–136
  common elements among, 119–123
  as communicators, 7–8
  contrast among, 123–128, 135–136, 170–171
  definition of, 2–3
  degree of convergence among, 136–139
  educational level, 9–10, 129–130
  efficiency, 123–124
  future, 164–176
  in global enterprises, 3–4, 27, 31
  goal setting, 120–121
  and government, 5–6
  job losses among, 15–16
  minority hiring by, 12–16
  as negotiators, 122
  personnel selection by, 121, 126–127
  promotion, 48, 57, 61–62, 130–132
  in public affairs, 144–146, 153–154, 158, 160–161, 173
  relations with other officers, 132–134
  responses to change, 6–8
  turnover, 127
  types of, 171–173
  understanding of environment, 120
  women, 11–12
Exxon, 66, 79

Feminists. *See* Women's movement
Filer, John, 151, 160
Filer Commission, 151
Financial services, 64, 66
  and computer technology, 4–5
Flexibility
  caution and, 173–175
  in union negotiations, 39
Foundations, private, 6, 147, 160
Friedman, Milton, 145, 152
Function, human resources, 56–76
  compensation in, 58, 63, 67
  definitions for, 58–59
  future of, 65–67

leadership role for, 71–75
performance superiority attitude, 67–69
philosophy of, 60–62
role problems, 62–65
self-management philosophy, 69–71
staffing for, 69–71
unfulfilled promise of, 167–169

Gade, Marian L., 131n
Gardner, John W., 133n, 134n
General Electric, 60, 66, 79
General Motors, 66, 78–79, 113
Generational differences among executives, 135, 170–171
GI Bill, 83
Global sourcing, 43, 48
Goal setting, 120–121
Golden handshakes, 88, 169
"Gospel of Wealth, The," 147
Government
  executives, 118, 123–128, 130, 134, 137–139
  growth, 147–148
  impact on economy, 5–6
  relations with business, 113, 137, 148, 154–157
  spending on social programs, 149
Great Depression, 135
Greenmail, 65
Greenwalt, Crawford, 81
Gronowski, John A., 139
Growth
  of government, 147–148
  industrial, 80, 83–86, 97
Harvard Business School, 129
Headquarters level, corporate strategy at, 46–50
Health Systems Agency, 78
Helstein, Ralph, 132
High school graduates, 8–9, 72, 83
  minority, 13–14
Hiring freeze, 85–87
Hispanics, 12, 14–15
Howard, A., 101n
Human resources
  and changing values, 16–17
  dimensions of, 38–39
  function, 56–76, 167–169
  in historical perspective, 35–40
  in large corporations, 20–32
  management studies, 100–112